FAILING TO CONFRONT ISLAMIC TOTALITARIANISM
FROM GEORGE W. BUSH TO BARACK OBAMA AND BEYOND

ONKAR GHATE AND ELAN JOURNO

WITH ADDITIONAL CONTRIBUTIONS BY
LEONARD PEIKOFF, YARON BROOK
AND KEITH LOCKITCH

AYN RAND
INSTITUTE PRESS

CONTENTS

INTRODUCTION

The present state of the world is not the proof of philosophy's impotence, but the proof of philosophy's power. It is philosophy that has brought men to this state—it is only philosophy that can lead them out.

— Ayn Rand, 1961

Look around the world, and you will see something that would have shocked anyone living in the aftermath of 9/11. Following the worst attack on American soil since Pearl Harbor, with thousands of our citizens killed, Americans were rightly outraged—and their (healthy) response was to demand retaliation. Our leaders in Washington insisted that the people who attacked us would be made to pay. No longer would anyone dare think of the United States as a "paper tiger." The prevailing mood conveyed a clear message: America was entitled to defend itself. The nation was primed to unleash its full military might to annihilate the threat.

Now consider just *some* of the brazen attacks in the last year and a half: the massacre at the Paris office of the magazine *Charlie Hebdo*; shootings at free-speech events in Copenhagen and in Garland, Texas; the suicide bombings and murder spree across Paris; the mass shooting in San Bernardino, California; the bombing of the Brussels airport and subway; the slaughter at a gay nightclub in Orlando, Florida.

The events of the last year and a half reflect a long-standing trend, one that was supercharged in the last decade and a half: the ascent of the Islamist cause. That movement is strong materially, capable of inflicting harm, controlling territory, subjugating people. And, what's more significant: the movement is strong in its morale, exhibiting an astounding confidence. Iran's state-backing for jihadist groups (according to the U.S. State Department) is "undiminished," and the regime seeks nuclear capability. Five-plus years after bin Laden's death, the al-Qaeda network lives on. The Taliban in Afghanistan has reconquered about as much territory as it held prior to the U.S.-led war. Across the Middle East, the Islamic State rampages. The group has conquered parts of Iraq and Syria, and it has distinguished itself through unspeakable barbarity. You might expect that to put potential recruits off, but in fact Islamic State is a magnet for foreign fighters, including many from Europe and North America.

Let that sink in: *Since 9/11, countless individuals have eagerly enlisted to fight for the cause of Islamic totalitarianism.*

At the same time, many Americans are exhausted, resigned, demoralized. Our military forces—mighty, brave, determined—were sent into Afghanistan and Iraq, two winnable wars that became quagmires. Materially, the Islamists are far weaker than the enemies we faced in World War II. Then, we eliminated the threat to our lives and freedom in less than five years. Since 9/11, however, we've been told that this must be a "long war." George W. Bush viewed Afghanistan and Iraq as unwinnable. Indeed, Afghanistan is the longest war in America's history. Barack Obama further scaled back expectations, pointedly ruling out a World War II-like "victory" (a word he feels uncomfortable using).

We have reached a new normal: clouding our daily lives is the persistent threat of jihadist attacks. And, for fear of incurring the wrath of Islamists, many newspapers, magazines, and publishing houses (such as Yale University Press and Random House) engage in self-censorship. What we're seeing is the twilight of the freedom of speech.

Suppose that in the wake of 9/11 you told people that this grim reality lay ahead. They would have been astounded. Indignant even. Some might have dismissed it as far-fetched. After all, our military strength is unmatched in all of world history. And yet, far from defeated, Islamic totalitarianism is on the march. No one would have predicted the situation we face today.

We at the Ayn Rand Institute predicted it.

We warned against precisely that kind of disaster. We pinpointed the fundamental problem subverting American foreign policy. We championed an uncompromising solution.

In the aftermath of 9/11, ARI placed full-page ads in the *Washington Post* and the *New York Times* explaining the attack and presenting an incisive warning. The "greatest obstacle to U.S. victory," wrote ARI's founder Leonard Peikoff, is not our enemies, but "our own intellectuals." They advocated the same ideas that had encouraged the enemy. "Fifty years of increasing American appeasement in the Mideast have led to fifty years of increasing contempt in the Muslim world for the U.S.," wrote Peikoff. The irrational ideas shaping American foreign policy had led to 9/11, and every indication pointed to one conclusion: those dominant ideas, unless rejected, would subvert the U.S. military response and our national security. America is a military superpower, but it lacks the self-confidence and moral certainty needed to understand and fight for its own self-defense.

Tragically our analysis—articulated in countless ARI op-eds, essays, media interviews, talks—has proved correct.

We argued that properly conceptualizing the enemy—identifying its character, its goals—is necessary in order to defeat it. Our enemy is defined, not primarily by their use of terrorist means, but by their ideological ends. They fight to create a society dominated by Islamic religious law. We call the movement Islamic totalitarianism—a cause long inspired and funded by patrons such as Saudi Arabia, the Gulf states and, above all, Iran. Yet the last two administrations not only failed to define the enemy, but evaded this responsibility. Witness the destructive consequences all around you. Over time the necessity of understanding the enemy has only grown more urgent.

We argued that a proper war is one fought in self-defense to safeguard the individual rights of Americans. We argued that such a war must seek to eliminate the objective threats to our lives, using all necessary force. Yet Bush's supposedly "muscular" policy was in fact animated by "compassion" and the allegedly moral ideal of selfless service to the needy. That's true of the overarching goal of Bush's crusade for democracy—giving the needy and oppressed of the Middle East the vote—and of its implementation on the ground. Far from unleashing a "shock and awe" campaign, Washington engaged in "nation building" and subjected our soldiers to absurd, self-sacrificial battlefield constraints. Those same constraints on our soldiers—stemming from the doctrines of Just War Theory and embodied in international norms of war—persist under Obama's administration.

We identified the predictable consequences of the ideas shaping America's foreign policy. Our forward-looking assessments were proven correct.

The democracy crusade, we argued, would empower jihadists across the Middle East. It did; see Iraq, Afghanistan, Lebanon, Egypt, the Palestinian territories.

On the battlefield the self-effacing rules of engagement, we argued, would encourage the Iraq insurgency and the remnants of the Taliban. They did.

We argued that the widely celebrated "surge" in Iraq—deploying thousands more U.S. soldiers to quell the insurgency through bribes and appeasing gestures—could only paper over, not end, the fundamental enmities and that more violence would return. It did.

Allowing insurgents to go undefeated, we warned, would enable the most vicious, effective killers to survive and reemerge. They did; one such insurgent group became the core of Islamic State.

The policy of appeasement, we argued, would only empower such enemies as Hamas and Hezbollah. It did; witness the Islamist-Israeli wars in 2006, 2008/9, 2012, 2014.

We argued that the prevailing response to the Danish cartoons crisis was pathetic. The West's inability to uphold so vital a right as the freedom of speech, we warned, would further inspire the jihadists. It did; recall *Charlie Hebdo*.

The diplomatic outreach to Iran, begun under Bush and consummated by Obama's team, would further encourage the standard bearer of the jihad, the Iranian regime; a nuclear deal—we warned a decade before it was signed—would fuel Iran's hostility. It did.

From the outset, we at ARI spelled out what a real war actually looks like; we highlighted the sharp contrast between that and the supposedly "tough" policy of the Bush administration in Iraq and Afghanistan. The wrong lesson, we warned, would be to regard Bush's (policy) failure as discrediting the use of military force in self-defense. That misconception, however, is now pervasive. Many (wrongly) believe that our military—despite being unrivaled—is ineffectual and, if used, counterproductive. We warned that that insidious premise was leading America to disarm itself, even as threats mount. And indeed that premise goes a long way to explaining how Obama's nuclear deal with Iran was seen as even remotely plausible. Obama posed the alternatives as another Middle East war—*another Iraq*—or the Iran deal. If "war" means another quagmire, everyone should reject it.

From the outset, we at ARI exposed the perverse ideas about morality that permeated, and therefore subverted, U.S. foreign policy. We warned that by subordinating military victory to allegedly moral constraints, Washington's policy would undermine our national security. The ruinous consequences of that policy abound.

What makes ARI's approach distinctive—and why our analysis has been borne out—is the intellectual framework that we embrace: Ayn Rand's philosophy of Objectivism. Thus our work fits in none of the conventional categories, such as conservative, libertarian, progressive, "realist", "isolationist," neoconservative. That ARI's perspective on U.S. foreign policy has been borne out is a testament to the real-world value of our philosophic framework. Objectivism begins by embracing a basic orientation to facts; *reality is*, and in the quest to live we must use our reason to discover reality's nature and learn to act successfully in it. The philosophy's moral code teaches us what is in our self-interest, what produces happiness, and what a proper society looks like. Rand once explained: "I am not primarily an advocate of capitalism, but of egoism; and I am not primarily an advocate of egoism, but of reason. If one recognizes the supremacy of reason and applies it consistently, all the rest follows." It is this philosophic outlook that led us to identify and take seriously the threat of Islamic totalitarianism, and then properly conceive what actions our self-defense required.

When looking at the cultural and political events of the day, we at ARI view them in a wider context, we identify issues in fundamental terms, and we recognize the profound role of philosophic ideas in shaping the world. We take our function to be in line with Ayn Rand's conception of the proper role of intellectuals in society: "The intellectual is the eyes, ears and voice of a free society: it is his job to observe the events of the world, to evaluate their meaning and to inform the men in all the other fields." This is the role all of ARI's intellectuals—whether writing on philosophy, foreign policy, law, economic issues—seek to live up to everyday, whereas our culture's leading intellectual voices have long ago abandoned it.

The major presentation of our view of what went wrong after 9/11 is *Winning the Unwinnable War: America's Self-Crippled Response to Islamic Totalitarianism*, edited by Elan Journo. In that book of in-depth essays, we show how conventional, dominant ideas about morality subverted American security.

The present book *echoes* that theme, but it conveys ARI's distinctive philosophic viewpoint in bite-size portions. In the op-eds, essays, blog posts, and interviews that we selected for inclusion here, you will see how irrational philosophic ideas warped foreign-policy thinking and crippled us in action. The argument laid out in *Winning the Unwinnable War* focuses on the George W. Bush administration, and part 1 of this book spans that period. Parts 2 through 4 cover the Obama years. That wider scope, subsuming two quite different administrations, only serves to underscore the profound impact of philosophic ideas in foreign policy, regardless of who sits in the Oval Office. You will also learn that victory is achievable—if we take certain necessary steps (a detailed account can be found in *Winning the Unwinnable War*). Part 5 sketches out how an Objectivist approach to foreign policy stands apart in today's intellectual landscape.

We at ARI fight for a future of reason, individualism, and freedom. We ask you to join us. How? The book's final section, "What You Can Do," provides concrete suggestions. Read, watch, listen to the recommended ARI content—then distribute it to others and speak up for your ideas and values.

Join us, and your support will multiply ARI's impact and fuel our mission. We make people aware of the philosophy of Objectivism because we believe that Objectivism is indispensable for understanding the world, defining values, and achieving one's own happiness. To convey that, we educate people about Rand's philosophy and we spotlight Objectivism's cash value in an individual's life and in society. From that philosophic perspective, we write and speak about crucial political-cultural issues of the day. What you'll find in the pages that follow is that the arena of U.S. foreign policy offers stark, life-and-death illustrations of the value of Objectivism for understanding the world and guiding our action.

Can we end the Islamist menace and secure our right to life, liberty, and the pursuit of happiness on earth? Yes—easily—if we adopt the right ideas.

ELAN JOURNO   ONKAR GHATE

"END STATES WHO SPONSOR TERRORISM"

Leonard Peikoff October 2, 2001

The following article appeared as a full-page advertisement in the *New York Times*.

Fifty years of increasing American appeasement in the Mideast have led to fifty years of increasing contempt in the Muslim world for the U.S. The climax was September 11, 2001.

Fifty years ago, Truman and Eisenhower surrendered the West's property rights in oil, although that oil rightfully belonged to those in the West whose science, technology, and capital made its discovery and use possible. The first country to nationalize Western oil, in 1951, was Iran. The rest, observing our frightened silence, hurried to grab their piece of the newly available loot.

The cause of the U.S. silence was not practical, but philosophical. The Mideast's dictators were denouncing wealthy egotistical capitalism. They were crying that their poor needed our sacrifice; that oil, like all property, is owned collectively, by virtue of birth; and that they knew their viewpoint was true by means of otherworldly emotion. Our Presidents had no answer. Implicitly, they were ashamed of the Declaration of Independence. They did not dare to answer that Americans, properly, were motivated by the selfish desire to achieve personal happiness in a rich, secular, individualist society.

The Muslim countries embodied in an extreme form every idea—selfless duty, anti-materialism, faith or feeling above science, the supremacy of the group—which our universities, our churches, and our own political Establishment had long been upholding as virtue. When two groups, our leadership and theirs, accept the same basic ideas, the most consistent side wins.

After property came liberty. "The Muslim fundamentalist movement," writes Yale historian Lamin Sanneh, "began in 1979 with the Iranian [theocratic] revolution . . ." (*New York Times*, 9/23/01). During his first year as its leader, Ayatollah Khomeini, urging a Jihad against "the Great Satan," kidnapped fifty-two U.S. diplomatic personnel and held them hostage; Carter's reaction was fumbling paralysis. About a decade later, Iran topped this evil. Khomeini issued his infamous

Fatwa aimed at censoring, even outside his borders, any ideas uncongenial to Muslim sensibility. This was the meaning of his threat to kill British author Rushdie and to destroy his American publisher; their crime was the exercise of their right to express an unpopular intellectual viewpoint. The Fatwa was Iran's attempt, reaffirmed after Khomeini's death, to stifle, anywhere in the world, the very process of thought. Bush Sr. looked the other way.

After liberty came American life itself. The first killers were the Palestinian hijackers of the late 1960s. But the killing spree which has now shattered our soaring landmarks, our daily routine, and our souls, began in earnest only after the license granted by Carter and Bush Sr.

Many nations work to fill our body bags. But Iran, according to a State Department report of 1999, is "the most active state sponsor of terrorism," training and arming groups from all over the Mideast, including Islamic Jihad, Hamas, and Hezbollah. Nor is Iran's government now "moderating." Five months ago, the world's leading terrorist groups resolved to unite in a holy war against the U.S., which they called "a second Israel"; their meeting was held in Tehran. (Fox News, 9/16/01)

What has been the U.S. response to the above? In 1996, nineteen U.S. soldiers were killed in their barracks in Saudi Arabia. According to a front-page story in the *New York Times* (6/21/98): "Evidence suggesting that Iran sponsored the attack has further complicated the investigation, because the United States and Saudi Arabia have recently sought to improve relations with a new, relatively moderate Government in Teheran." In other words, Clinton evaded Iran's role because he wanted what he called "a genuine reconciliation." In public, of course, he continued to vow that he would find and punish the guilty. This inaction of Clinton's is comparable to his action after bin Laden's attack on U.S. embassies in East Africa; his action was the gingerly bombing of two meaningless targets.

Conservatives are equally responsible for today's crisis, as Reagan's record attests. Reagan not only failed to retaliate after 241 U.S. marines in Lebanon were slaughtered; he did worse. Holding that Islamic guerrillas were our ideological allies because of their fight against the atheistic Soviets, he methodically poured money and expertise into Afghanistan. This put the U.S. wholesale into the business of creating terrorists. Most of them regarded fighting the Soviets as only the beginning; our turn soon came.

For over a decade, there was another guarantee of American impotence: the notion that a terrorist is alone responsible for his actions, and that each, therefore, must be tried as an individual before a court of law. This viewpoint, thankfully, is fading; most people now understand that terrorists exist only through the sanction and support of a government.

We need not prove the identity of any of these creatures, because terrorism is not an issue of personalities. It cannot be stopped by destroying bin Laden and the al-Qaeda army, or even by destroying the destroyers everywhere. If that is all we do, a new army of militants will soon rise up to replace the old one.

The behavior of such militants is that of the regimes which make them possible. Their atrocities are not crimes, but acts of war. The proper response, as the public now understands, is a war in self-defense. In the excellent words of Paul Wolfowitz, deputy secretary of defense, we must "end states who sponsor terrorism."

A proper war in self-defense is one fought without self-crippling restrictions placed on our commanders in the field. It must be fought with the most effective weapons we possess (a few weeks ago, Rumsfeld refused, correctly, to rule out nuclear weapons). And it must be fought in a manner that secures victory as quickly as possible and with the fewest U.S. casualties, regardless of the countless innocents caught in the line of fire. These innocents suffer and die because of the action of their own government in sponsoring the initiation of force against America. Their fate, therefore, is their government's moral responsibility. There is no way for our bullets to be aimed only at evil men.

The public understandably demands retaliation against Afghanistan. But in the wider context Afghanistan is insignificant. It is too devastated even to breed many fanatics. Since it is no more these days than a place to hide, its elimination would do little to end terrorism.

Terrorism is a specific disease, which can be treated only by a specific antidote. The nature of the disease (though not of its antidote) has been suggested by Serge Schmemann (*New York Times*, 9/16/01). Our struggle now, he writes, is "not a struggle against a conventional guerrilla force, whose yearning for a national homeland or the satisfaction of some grievance could be satisfied or denied. The terrorists [on Tuesday] . . . issued no demands, no ultimatums. They did it solely out of grievance and hatred—hatred for the values cherished in the West as freedom, tolerance, prosperity, religious pluralism and universal suffrage, but abhorred by religious fundamentalists (and not only Muslim fundamentalists) as licentiousness, corruption, greed and apostasy."

Every word of this is true. The obvious implication is that the struggle against terrorism is not a struggle over Palestine. It is a clash of cultures, and thus a struggle of ideas, which can be dealt with, ultimately, only by intellectual means. But this fact does not depreciate the crucial role of our armed forces. On the contrary, it increases their effectiveness, by pointing them to the right target.

Most of the Mideast is ruled by thugs who would be paralyzed by an American victory over any of their neighbors. Iran, by contrast, is the only major country there ruled by zealots dedicated not to material gain (such as more wealth or territory), but to the triumph by any means, however violent, of the Muslim fundamentalist movement they brought to life. That is why Iran manufactures the most terrorists.

If one were under a Nazi aerial bombardment, it would be senseless to restrict oneself to combatting Nazi satellites while ignoring Germany and the ideological plague it was working to spread. What Germany was to Nazism in the 1940s, Iran is to terrorism today. Whatever else it does, therefore, the U.S. can put an end to the Jihadmongers only by taking out Iran.

Eliminating Iran's terrorist sanctuaries and military capability is not enough. We must do the equivalent of de-Nazifying the country, by expelling every official and bringing down every branch of its government. This goal cannot be achieved painlessly, by weaponry alone. It requires invasion by ground troops, who will be at serious risk, and perhaps a period of occupation. But nothing less will "end the state" that most cries out to be ended.

The greatest obstacle to U.S. victory is not Iran and its allies, but our own intellectuals. Even now, they are advocating the same ideas that caused our historical paralysis. They are asking a reeling nation to show neighbor-love by shunning "vengeance." The multiculturalists—rejecting the concept of objectivity—are urging us to "understand" the Arabs and avoid "racism" (i.e., any condemnation of any group's culture). The friends of "peace" are reminding us, ever more loudly, to "remember Hiroshima" and beware the sin of pride.

These are the kinds of voices being heard in the universities, the churches, and the media as the country recovers from its first shock, and the professoriate et al. feel emboldened to resume business as usual. These voices are a siren song luring us to untroubled sleep while the fanatics proceed to gut America.

Tragically, Mr. Bush is attempting a compromise between the

people's demand for a decisive war and the intellectuals' demand for appeasement.

It is likely that the Bush administration will soon launch an attack on bin Laden's organization in Afghanistan and possibly even attack the Taliban. Despite this, however, every sign indicates that Mr. Bush will repeat the mistakes made by his father in Iraq. As of October 1, the Taliban leadership appears not to be a target. Even worse, the administration refuses to target Iran, or any of the other countries identified by the State Department as terrorist regimes. On the contrary, Powell is seeking to add to the current coalition these very states—which is the equivalent of going into partnership with the Soviet Union in order to fight Communism (under the pretext, say, of proving that we are not anti-Russian). By seeking such a coalition, our President is asserting that he needs the support of terrorist nations in order to fight them. He is stating publicly that the world's only super-power does not have enough self-confidence or moral courage to act unilaterally in its own defense.

For some days now, Mr. Bush has been downplaying the role of our military, while praising the same policies (mainly negotiation and economic pressure) that have failed so spectacularly and for so long. Instead of attacking the roots of global terrorism, he seems to be settling for a "guerrilla war" against al-Qaeda, and a policy of unseating the Taliban passively, by aiding a motley coalition of native tribes. Our battle, he stresses, will be a "lengthy" one.

Mr. Bush's compromise will leave the primary creators of terrorism whole—and unafraid. His approach might satisfy our short-term desire for retribution, but it will guarantee catastrophe in the long term.

As yet, however, no overall policy has been solidified; the administration still seems to be groping. And an angry public still expects our government not merely to hobble terrorism for a while, but to eradicate it. The only hope left is that Mr. Bush will listen to the public, not to the professors and their progeny.

When should we act, if not now? If our appeasement has led to an escalation of disasters in the past, can it do otherwise in the future? Do we wait until our enemies master nuclear, chemical, and biological warfare?

The survival of America is at stake. The risk of a U.S. overreaction, therefore, is negligible. The only risk is underreaction.

Mr. Bush must reverse course. He must send our missiles and

troops, in force, where they belong. And he must justify this action by declaring with righteous conviction that we have discarded the clichés of our paper-tiger past and that the U.S. now places America first.

There is still time to demonstrate that we take the war against terrorism seriously—as a sacred obligation to our Founding Fathers, to every victim of the men who hate this country, and to ourselves. There is still time to make the world understand that we will take up arms, anywhere and on principle, to secure an American's right to life, liberty, and the pursuit of happiness on earth.

The choice today is mass death in the United States or mass death in the terrorist nations. Our Commander-In-Chief must decide whether it is his duty to save Americans or the governments who conspire to kill them.

PART 1

The Self-Crippled Response

Innocents in War?

Onkar Ghate January 18, 2002

If President Bush makes the solemn decision to go to war with Iraq in self-defense, he must not shackle our nation—as he did in Afghanistan—with his own personal religious or altruistic notions. As president, he has no right to worry about civilian causalities in enemy territory. As president, his chosen obligation is to achieve U.S. victory while safeguarding the lives of each and every one of the courageous individuals who have volunteered to defend America.

The government of a free nation is simply the agent of its citizens, charged with one fundamental responsibility: to secure the individual rights—and very lives—of its citizens through the use of retaliatory force. An aspect of this responsibility is to uphold each citizen's right to self-defense, a responsibility our government in part meets by eliminating terrorist states that threaten U.S. citizens.

If, however, in waging war our government considers the deaths of civilians in terrorist states as a cost that must be weighed against the deaths of our own soldiers (or civilians), or as a cost that must be weighed against achieving victory over the enemy, our government thereby violates its most basic function. It becomes not an agent for our self-defense, but theirs.

Morally, the U.S. government must destroy our aggressors by whatever means are necessary and minimize U.S. casualties in the process.

To be victorious in war, a free nation has to destroy enough of the aggressor to break his will to continue attacking (and, then, dismantle his war apparatus and, where necessary, replace his government). In modern warfare, this almost always necessitates "collateral damage," i.e., the killing of civilians.

In fact, victory with a minimum of one's own casualties sometimes requires a free nation to deliberately target the civilians of an aggressor nation in order to cripple its economic production and/or break its will. This is what the U.S. did in WWII when it dropped fire bombs on Dresden and Hamburg and atomic bombs on Hiroshima and Nagasaki. These bombings were moral acts. The destruction of Hiroshima and Nagasaki, for instance, precipitated Japan's surrender and so achieved victory with no further U.S. casualties. In that context, to sacrifice the lives of hundreds of thousands of U.S. soldiers in a ground attack on Japan would have been morally monstrous.

But, it will be objected, is it not more monstrous to kill all those innocent civilians?

No. The moral principle is: the responsibility for all deaths in war lies with the aggressor who initiates force, not with those who defend themselves. (Similarly, if in self-defense you shoot a hit man about to kill you, and also strike the innocent bystander the hit man was deliberately using as a shield, moral responsibility for the bystander's death lies with the hit man not you.)

Moreover, the objection contains a mistaken assumption: it is false that every civilian in enemy territory—whether we are speaking of Hitler's Germany or Hirohito's Japan or the Taliban's Afghanistan or Hussein's Iraq—is innocent.

Many civilians in the Middle East, for example, hate us and actively support, materially and/or spiritually, those plotting our deaths. Can one seriously maintain, for instance, that the individuals in the Middle East who celebrated by dancing in the streets on September 11 are innocent?

Other civilians in enemy states are passive, unthinking followers. Their work and economic production, however meager, supports their terrorist governments and so they are in part responsible for the continued power of our enemies. They too are not innocent—and their deaths may be unavoidable in order for America to defend itself. (Remember too that today's civilian is tomorrow's soldier.)

But what of those who truly are innocent?

The civilians in enemy territory who actually oppose their dictatorial, terrorist governments are usually their governments' first innocent victims. All such individuals who remain alive and outside of prison camps should try to flee their country or fight with us (as some did in Afghanistan).

And the truly innocent who live in countries that initiate force against other nations will acknowledge the moral right of a free nation to bomb their countries and destroy their governments—even if this jeopardizes their own lives. No truly innocent civilian in Nazi Germany, for example, would have questioned the morality of the Allies razing Germany, even if he knew he may die in the attacks. No truly innocent individual wishes to become a tool of or a shield for his murderous government; he wishes to see his government toppled.

Thus it should be unsurprising that a European think tank reported last year that "a significant number of those Iraqis interviewed, with surprising candor, expressed their view that, if [regime change] required an American-led attack, they would support it."

As a free nation our goal is our own defense, not civilian deaths, but we must not allow human shields, innocent or otherwise, to deter us from defending ourselves.

The U.S. government recognized the truth of this on September 11 when, in order to defend those citizens it could, it ordered the shooting down of any more airplanes-become-missiles, even though this meant killing not only the terrorists but also the innocent American civilians captive onboard.

The government must now recognize that the same principle applies to civilian captives in Iraq and the rest of the Middle East.

War is terrible but sometimes necessary. To win the war on terrorism, we must not let a mistaken concern with "innocents" deter us. As a free nation, we have the moral right to defend ourselves, even if this requires mass civilian casualties in terrorist countries.

America Is Not Winning the War

Onkar Ghate August 29, 2002

As we pause on September 11 to remember the stockbrokers, police-men, firefighters and many other fallen Americans, it is vital also to reflect on the progress of the war. For it was precisely to prevent future September 11ths that America responded with force. How goes the war?

Tragically, not well.

To wage a war in self-defense you must know who your enemy is. But our enemy remains unidentified and, therefore, untargeted. Ours is a war against "terrorism"—a form of violence, not an ideological opponent intent on killing us. Our enemies, however, are dedicated to a fundamentalist interpretation of Islam, which extols faith, mindless obedience, sacrifice to state and God, primitivism, theocracy. This is why they are at war with the "Great Satan," America, the foremost embodiment of the opposite values: reason, individualism, the selfish pursuit of happiness, secularism, capitalism. bin Laden understands this: "Hostility toward America," he declares, "is a religious duty." But our politicians, schooled in pragmatism and range-of-the-moment non-thinking, cannot conceive of an ideologically motivated conflict. An individual terrorist brandishing a bomb, like bin Laden, may still be real to them, but the movement for which he fights, Islamic fundamentalism, is not. Thus, we try to kill a few terrorists—but leave untouched the main militant Islamic states breeding the terrorists. We have no long-term plan to achieve victory in the war because we cannot identify the enemy that must be incapacitated. Ask yourself: Would America have been victorious in WWII if our goal had been to destroy "kamikaze-ism," not Japanese totalitarianism?

Worse, to the extent that our policy makers glimpse the mystical ideology operative in the Middle East, they consider it a positive force. As pragmatists, they are intellectually blind to the historical evidence of centuries of religious wars and are led, instead, by their own religious feelings. They can grasp no connection between faith taken seriously as the ruling principle of every aspect of man's life—and the attempt to physically force such dogma on nonbelievers. The terrorists,

---

This article originally appeared in the *Greenville News*.

on this approach, are inexplicable aberrations, deluded interpreters of true faith, who, mysteriously, try to spread their mystical doctrines by appeal not to a rational argument but to a gun. We therefore treat as allies such enemies of reason as Saudi Arabia, which spawns Islamic fundamentalists and finances their suicide bombers, and Pakistan, which trained the Taliban and punishes blasphemy with death. Our government even courts Iran, the spearhead of militant Islamic fundamentalism, and works with Iranian officials to foster "religious values" at U.N. conferences.

Predictably, the administration's actions, guided as they are not by reason but by emotion (including emotions of outrage), are chaotic and contradictory. No one knows what—if anything—America will do next in the war because we ourselves don't know what we'll do or why. Bush pays lip service to the correct idea that you are either for America's ideals or against them, but undermines our strongest ally in the war, Israel. He even promises the Palestinians a provisional state, thereby teaching every would-be killer that to the terrorist go the spoils. In typically empty rhetoric Bush declares that there is an axis of evil in the world, but allows Syria to head the U.N. Security Council and pursues dialogue with axis-of-evil-members North Korea and Iran—all terrorist states according to his own government.

Without actual principles, where will such a mentality turn for moral guidance? The answer is: to others and their moral views. So Bush—programmed by feelings formed from millennia of assertions that it is evil to uphold one's own interests, that the strong must sacrifice to the weak, that the meek shall inherit the earth—undercuts any genuine action taken in America's self-defense. In Afghanistan, for instance, morally unsure of his right to safeguard American lives, Bush feared world disapproval over civilian casualties. He would neither commit the number of American ground troops required to capture the enemy nor authorize the kind of massive bombing necessary to kill the enemy before it fled. The result: hundreds of Taliban and al-Qaeda escaped to plot further American destruction. In the Middle East, uncertain of America's right unilaterally to defend its interests, the administration obsesses with "coalition-building" (which includes shunning Israel and courting Saudi Arabia) and refuses to proclaim the superiority of America's ideals over those of medieval barbarism.

Lacking the moral conviction to uphold its values abroad, America increasingly and self-destructively turns inward, shifting its focus to such relatively trivial questions as whether airline pilots should be armed or government bureaucracies reshuffled. Because of our inaction on foreign soil, we resign ourselves to more terrorist attacks like that of September 11.

How then goes the war? An objective answer must be: badly. But our cause is not yet lost. We lack not the wealth nor the skilled military necessary to defeat the enemy, only the ideas and the will. If we articulate and practice a rational foreign policy, one actually premised on America's self-interest, we will prevail. Nothing more is needed to achieve victory than to replace the pragmatism and self-sacrifice now dictating America's actions with the principles of reason and rational self-interest; nothing less will do.

Don't Blame Our Intelligence Agencies— Blame Our Unprincipled Foreign Policy

Onkar Ghate April 2, 2004

The 900-page congressional report criticizing the operations of the FBI and CIA in the months prior to the September 11 attacks misses the fundamental point. Whatever incompetence on the intelligence agencies' part, what made September 11 possible was a failure, not by our intelligence agencies—but by the accommodating, range-of-the-moment, unprincipled foreign policy that has shaped our government's decisions for decades.

September 11 was not the first time America was attacked by Islamic fundamentalists engaged in "holy war" against us. In 1979 theocratic Iran—which has spearheaded the "Islamic Revolution"—stormed the U.S. embassy in Tehran and held fifty-two Americans hostage for over a year. In 1983 the Syrian- and Iranian-backed group Hezbollah bombed a U.S. marine barracks in Lebanon, killing 241 servicemen while they slept; the explosives came from Yasser Arafat's Fatah movement. In 1998 al-Qaeda blew up the U.S. embassies in Kenya and Tanzania, killing 224 individuals. In 2000 al-Qaeda bombed the USS *Cole* in Yemen, killing seventeen sailors.

So we already knew that al-Qaeda was actively engaged in attacking Americans. We even had evidence that agents connected to al-Qaeda had been responsible for the 1993 bombing of the World Trade Center. And we knew in 1996 that bin Laden had made an overt declaration of war against the "Satan" America.

But how did America react? Did our government adopt a principled approach and identify the fact that we were faced with a deadly threat from an ideological foe? Did we launch systematic counterattacks to wipe out such enemy organizations as al-Qaeda, Hezbollah and Fatah? Did we seek to eliminate enemy states like Iran? No—our responses were short-sighted and self-contradictory.

For instance, we initially expelled Iranian diplomats—but later sought an appeasing rapprochement with that ayatollah-led government. We intermittently cut off trade with Iran—but secretly negotiated weapons-for-hostages deals. When Israel had the courage to enter

---

This article originally appeared in the *Providence Journal*.

Lebanon in 1982 to destroy the PLO, we refused to uncompromisingly support our ally and instead brokered the killers' release. And with respect to al-Qaeda, we dropped a perfunctory bomb or two on one of its suspected camps, while our compliant diplomats waited for al-Qaeda's terrorist attacks to fade from the headlines.

At home, we treated our attackers as if they were isolated criminals rather than soldiers engaged in battle against us. In 1941 we did not attempt to indict the Japanese pilots who bombed Pearl Harbor—we declared war on the source. Yet we spent millions trying to indict specific terrorists—while we ignored their masters.

Despite emphatic pronouncements from Islamic leaders about a "jihad" against America, our political leaders failed to grasp the ideology that seeks our destruction. This left them unable to target that enemy's armed combatants—in Palestine, Iran, Iraq, Syria, Saudi Arabia—and the governments that assist them. Is it any wonder then that, although our intelligence agencies prevented many planned attacks, they could not prevent them all?

Unfortunately, little has changed since September 11. Our politicians' actions remain hopelessly unprincipled. Despite the Bush administration's rhetoric about ending states that sponsor terrorism, President Bush has left the most dangerous of these—Iran—untouched. The attack on Iraq, though justifiable, was hardly a priority in our war against militant Islam and the countries (principally, Saudi Arabia and Iran) that promote it. Moreover, when Bush does strike at militant Islam, he does so only haltingly. Morally unsure of his right to protect American lives by wiping out the Taliban and al-Qaeda, Bush feared in Afghanistan world disapproval over civilian casualties. Consequently, he reined in the military forces (as he also did in Iraq) and allowed numerous Taliban and al-Qaeda fighters to escape. And Bush continues to allow their comrades in arms in the Middle East to go unharmed. He pretends that the Palestinians and Islamic militants attacking Israel—and who have attacked Americans in the past and will try again in the future—are, somehow, different from the killers in Afghanistan and deserving of a "peace" plan.

Instead of taking consistent, principled action to destroy our terrorist adversaries, politicians from both parties continue to focus on details like reshuffling government bureaucracies and haggling over how much criticism of Saudi Arabia the 900-page congressional report can contain. Thus, too unprincipled to identify the enemy and wage all-out war, but not yet completely blind to their own ineffectualness, our leaders resignedly admit that we're in for a "long war" and that there will be more terrorists attacks on U.S. soil.

There is only one way to prevent a future September 11: by rooting out the amoral, pragmatic expediency that now dominates our government's foreign policy.

America's Compassion in Iraq
Is Self-Destructive

Elan Journo and *Yaron Brook* January 12, 2005

The horrific suicide bombing in December of a U.S. mess tent near Mosul and the assassination on January 10 of the deputy chief of Baghdad police—the second Iraqi official murdered in five days—are further indications that the war in Iraq is worsening. Things are going badly not because, as some claim, the United States is arrogant and lacking in humility—but because it is self-effacing and compassionate.

The Bush administration's war in Iraq embraces compassion instead of the rational goal of victory. Such an immoral approach to war wantonly sacrifices the lives of soldiers and emboldens our enemies throughout the Middle East to mount further attacks against us.

Regardless of whether the Iraqi dictatorship should have been our initial target in the war against totalitarian Islam, when in the nation's defense a president sends troops to war, morally he must resolve to soundly defeat the enemy while safeguarding our forces and citizens. But America's attention has been diverted to rebuilding Iraqi hospitals, schools, roads and sewers, and on currying favor with the locals (some U.S. soldiers were even ordered to grow moustaches in token of their respect for Iraqi culture, others are now given cultural sensitivity courses before arriving in Iraq). Since the war began, Islamic militants and Saddam Hussein loyalists have carried out random abductions, devastating ambushes, and catastrophic bombings throughout the country. That attacks on U.S. forces (including those engaged in reconstruction efforts) have gone unpunished has emboldened the enemy.

Early and stark evidence of the enemy's growing audacity came in March 2004 with the grisly murder and mutilation of four American contractors. Following the attack, U.S. forces entered the city of Fallujah vowing to capture the murderers and punish the town that supports them. But such resolve was supplanted by compassion.

In the midst of the fighting, the United States called a unilateral ceasefire to allow humanitarian aid in and to enable the other side to collect and bury its dead. The so-called truce benefited only the enemy. The Iraqis, as one soldier told the Associated Press, were "absolutely taking advantage" of the situation, regrouping and mounting sporadic attacks: as another soldier aptly noted, "It is hard to have a cease-fire when they maneuver against us, they fire at us." As the siege wore on, the goal of capturing the murderers quietly faded—and the enemy's confidence swelled.

Neither the later offensive on Fallujah in November nor any of the subsequent incursions have quelled the insurgents: witness the unending string of car bombings and (roadside) ambushes. Why?

Because in Fallujah and throughout this war the military (under orders from Washington) has been purposely treading lightly. Soldiers have strict orders to avoid the risk of killing civilians—many of whom aid or are themselves militants—even at the cost of imperiling their own lives. Mosques, which have served as hideouts for terrorists, are kept off the list of allowed targets. Military operations have been timed to avoid alienating Muslim pilgrims on holy days.

There is no shortage of aggressors lusting for American blood, and they grow bolder with each display of American compassion.

Consider the shameful tenderness shown toward the Islamic cleric Moktadr al-Sadr, who aspires to be the dictator of an Iranian-style theocracy in Iraq. An admirer of the 9/11 hijackers, Sadr has amassed an armed militia of 10,000 men (right under the noses of our military), and demanded that Coalition forces leave Iraq. On the run for the murder of another cleric, he took refuge with his militia in the holy city of Najaf, which has been surrounded by U.S. troops. Rather than attacking, however, the United States agreed to negotiate. It is as absurd to negotiate with and trust the word of a villain such as Sadr as it would have been to negotiate with Nazis bent on wiping out Allied forces in World War II. It is shockingly dangerous that the United States allowed a mediator from Iran—part of the "Axis of Evil" and Sadr's ideological ally—to assist in the negotiations.

In the end Sadr was allowed to walk away, along with his armed militia; his agreement to disarm them has—predictably—gone unfulfilled.

For the enemies of America, Iraq is like a laboratory where they are testing our mettle, with mounting ferocity. The negotiations with Sadr; the half-hearted raids on Fallujah; our timid response to daily insurrections throughout Iraq; America's outrageously deferential treatment of its enemies—all of these instances of moral weakness reinforce the view of bin Laden and his ilk that America will appease those who seek its destruction.

If we continue to confess doubts about our moral right to defend ourselves, it will only be a matter of time before Islamic militants bring suicide bombings and mass murder (again) to the streets of the United States.

Though Washington may be blinded by the longing to buy the love of Iraqis, our servicemen know all too well that (as one put it): "When you go to fight, it's time to shoot—not to make friends with people." In its might and courage, our military is unequaled; it is the moral responsibility of Washington to issue battle plans that will properly "shock and awe" the enemy. Eschewing self-interest in the name of compassion is immoral. The result is self-destruction.

Bush's Betrayal of America:
The Iraqi Elections

Elan Journo January 28, 2005

President Bush claims that holding elections on January 30 will bring Iraq a step closer to freedom, an outcome allegedly vital to America's security. But the Iraqi election will bring neither freedom to Iraq nor security to America.

Consider the beliefs of the Iraqis who will be voting for "freedom" in the upcoming election. Like so many peoples in the Middle East, Iraqis regard themselves as defined by their membership in some larger group, not by their own ideas and goals. Most Iraqis owe their loyalties—and derive their honor from belonging—to their familial clan, tribe or religious sect, to which the individual is subservient. This deep-seated tribalism is reflected in the parties running in the elections: there is a spectrum ranging from advocates of secular collectivist ideologies (communists and Ba'athists) to those defined by bloodlines (such as Kurds and Turkmens) to members of various religious sects.

What will be the result of an election featuring such voters and candidates? Iraqis will merely bring to power some assortment of collectivists and Islamists. Whatever constitution those leaders eventually frame will reflect their desire to arrogate power to their particular group and to settle old scores, such as the longstanding enmity between the Shiite majority and the Sunnis. It may well permit barbaric treatment of individuals, commonly accepted throughout the Islamic world, such as "honor-killings" of women believed to have had sex before marriage, or the banning of "un-Islamic" speech. And in the long term, the new nation may become an active sponsor of Islamic terrorism.

Perhaps the most alarming outcome for U.S. security would be a popularly elected theocracy aligned with or highly sympathetic to Iran's totalitarian regime. Iran is reported to have smuggled nearly one million people into Iraq to vote and has donated millions of dollars to sway the election in favor of a Shiite-led government. Already, Iranian intelligence officials are said to roam the hallways of Iraqi party offices, on whose walls hang pictures of Iran's supreme leader.

That a theocracy may rise to power in Iraq appears to be totally compatible with the president's conception of "freedom." As he told

Fox News in October, if Iraq votes in a fundamentalist government, he would "be disappointed. But democracy is democracy. . . . If that's what the people choose, that's what the people choose."

This certainly is democracy—in its literal sense of unlimited majority rule. But it is not freedom.

Political freedom does not mean the expression of a collective will, nor the granting of power to one pressure group to exploit others. It means the protection of an individual from the initiation of physical force by others. Freedom rests on the idea of individualism: the principle that every man is an independent, sovereign being, that he is not an interchangeable fragment of the tribe; that his life, liberty and possessions are his by right, not by the permission of any group. Democracy (i.e., majority rule) rests on the primacy of the group; if your gang is strong enough, you can get away with whatever you want, sacrificing the life and wealth of whoever stands in your way. This is why America's Founders rejected democracy and created a republican form of government, limited by the inalienable rights of the smallest "minority": the individual. Our system does have elections, of course, but they are only legitimate within a constitutional framework that prohibits the majority from voting away the rights of anyone.

Can freedom be achieved in Iraq? In the near future, no—which is one of many reasons why it is suicidal for Bush to treat Iraqi freedom as the centerpiece of American self-defense. American security does not require that the terrorism-sponsoring nations of the Middle East be free, only that they be non-threatening—a goal that can be achieved by making it clear to the leaders of these nations that any continued sponsorship of terrorism will mean their immediate destruction.

In the long run, if Iraqis or other peoples of the Middle East are to become free—a task that is their responsibility, not America's—they must first recognize that their current ideas and practices are incompatible with freedom. They must recognize that they need to adopt a philosophy of individualism. A good first step toward teaching this lesson would be not granting them the pretense of elections.

The Foreign Policy of Guilt

Onkar Ghate and *Yaron Brook*   July 29, 2005

In the aftermath of the [July 7, 2005, suicide] bombings in London, Prime Minister Tony Blair has asked the British people to remain calm and maintain their daily routines; the terrorists win, he says, if one gives in to fear. This, you may remember, was also George W. Bush's response after September 11, when he called on Americans to return to our shopping malls and not be afraid.

But we should be afraid—precisely because of Blair's and Bush's policies.

We face an enemy, Islamic totalitarianism, committed to our deaths. Its agents have shown an eagerness to kill indiscriminately in London, Madrid, New York and elsewhere, even at the cost of their own lives. They continually seek chemical and nuclear weapons; imagine the death toll if such devices had been used in London's subway bombings. In the face of this mounting threat, what is our response?

Do we proudly proclaim our unconditional right to exist? Do we resolutely affirm to eradicate power base after power base of the Islamic totalitarians, until they drop their arms, and foreign governments and civilian populations no longer have the nerve to support them?

No. Blair's response to the London bombings, with Bush and the other members of the G8 by his side, was, in meaning if not in explicit statement, to apologize and do penance for our existence.

Somehow we in the West and not the Palestinians—with their rejection of the freedoms attainable in Israel and their embrace of thugs and killers—are responsible for their degradation. Thus, we must help build them up by supplying the terrorist-sponsoring Palestinian Authority with billions in aid. And somehow we in the West and not the Africans—with their decades of tribal, collectivist and anticapitalist ideas—are responsible for their poverty. Thus we must lift them out of their plight with $50 billion in aid. This, Blair claims, will help us "triumph over terrorism."

The campaigns in Afghanistan and Iraq might be considered exceptions to this orgy of penance, but that would be an error. In neither war was the aim to smash the enemy. Unlike in WWII, when the Allies would flatten cities to achieve victory, the American and British armies, by explicit order, tiptoed in the Middle East. Terrorists and

17

insurgents went free, free to return to kill our young men, because we subordinated the lives of our soldiers to concern for the enemy's well-being and civilian casualties. Our goal was not victory but, as Bush so often tells us, to bestow with our soldiers' blood an unearned gift on these people, "freedom" and "democracy," with the hope that they would then stop killing us.

According to Blair, our duty is to shower the globe with money. According to Bush, our duty is to shower the globe with "democracy." Taken together, the meaning of their foreign policy is clear. The West has no moral right to exist, because it is productive, prosperous and free; materially and spiritually, with its money and its soldiers' lives, the West must buy permission to exist from the rest of the world. But the rest of the world has an unquestionable right to exist, because it is unproductive, poor and unfree.

Until we in the West reject this monstrous moral premise, we will never have cause to feel safe.

What we desperately need is a leader who proclaims that the rational ideals of the West, reason, science, individual rights and capitalism, are good—that we have a moral right to exist for our own sake—that we don't owe the rest of the world anything—and that we should be admired and emulated for our virtues and accomplishments, not denounced. This leader would then demonstrate, in word and deed, that if those opposed to these ideals take up arms against us, they will be crushed.

Support for totalitarian Islam will wither only when the Islamic world is convinced that the West will fight—and fight aggressively. As long as the insurgents continue with their brutal acts in Iraq, unharmed by the mightiest military force in human history, as long as the citizens of London return to "normal" lives with subways exploding all around them, as long as the West continues to negotiate with Iran on nuclear weapons—as long as the West continues to appease its enemies, because it believes it has no moral right to destroy them, totalitarian Islam is emboldened.

It is the West's moral weakness that feeds terrorism and brings it fresh recruits. It is the prospect of success against the West, fueled by the West's apologetic response, that allows totalitarian Islam to thrive.

Bush has said repeatedly, in unguarded moments, that this war is un-winnable. By his foreign policy, it is. But if the British and American people gain the self-esteem to assert our moral right to exist—with everything this entails—victory will be ours.

The Perversity of U.S. Backing for the Gaza Retreat

Elan Journo August 30, 2005

In a step fraught with danger, Israel is uprooting its citizens and withdrawing its military from Gaza and parts of the West Bank. That Palestinian terrorists are rejoicing over this momentous pullout is hardly shocking. That the United States is also applauding is contemptible. Worse still, America is demanding more concessions of land: Secretary of State Rice has insisted, "It cannot be Gaza only."

Why is America urging Israel to make such perilous concessions? The rationale is that the withdrawal will open an unobstructed path for the "downtrodden" Palestinians toward a self-governed ethnic state. Such a state, Washington hopes, will alleviate their suffering and establish peaceful co-existence between Israel and the Palestinians.

But such a state will intensify the misery of the few genuinely freedom-seeking Palestinians by entrenching a tyrannical regime. The Palestinian Authority, a provisional governing body, has drained the lifeblood out of its citizens, trampled on their rights and, despite receiving billions in foreign aid, kept them in devastating poverty. Under the PA's anarchic reign, rival "security forces" arbitrarily seize property, arrest and jail people without charge, and summarily execute dissidents.

The actual victors of the withdrawal are terrorists and their vast legions of reverent supporters in the Palestinian population. The motto emblazoned on banners throughout Gaza expresses their belief, borne out in practice, that violence works: "Gaza Today. The West Bank and Jerusalem Tomorrow." The withdrawal has strengthened their resolve, not to achieve peace, but to destroy Israel. "We're going to keep our weapons," one terrorist told reporters, "because the battle with the enemy is a long one." A cleric allied to Hamas, which has carried out umpteen suicide bombings in Israel, observed that "when we offer up our children [as 'martyrs'], it is much better than choosing the road of humiliation and negotiations."

This article originally appeared in *Capitalism Magazine*.

As some have observed, with a populace and leadership so hospitable to terrorists, in time the Palestinian territories may succeed Taliban-ruled Afghanistan as a training ground for jihadists, lusting to murder not only in the streets of Jerusalem and Baghdad, but also London and New York.

Israel's retreat from Gaza—rightly celebrated by terrorists—is neither a means of fostering peace, nor a solution for the plight of innocent Palestinians. Why, then, does America support it?

Because Washington holds that Israel has no moral right to assert its interests, but the Palestinians do. Their quest for statehood enjoys Washington's wholehearted support, encouragement and financing as an incontestable entitlement—even if they tyrannize themselves and terrorize Israel. But if Israel pursues its interests, by contrast, Washington considers that a moral transgression. Israel could, and for a time did, easily protect the lives and property of all individuals within its borders and the contested territories, by smashing aggressors and imposing its rule of law on Palestinians (which innocent Palestinians welcomed). But Washington refuses on principle to endorse such assertions of Israeli interests.

Why this double standard? Our leaders believe in altruism: the view that one's highest moral duty is to selflessly serve the needy—and thus that the world's "haves" must sacrifice for the sake of its "have-nots." The productive, on this abhorrent view, have no moral right to pursue their own interests; their only justification for existing is to serve the needy. Because Israel is strong and prosperous, it is thereby forbidden from imposing its will on the destitute Palestinians—even though it is the innocent victim of Palestinian aggression. Because the Palestinians are weak and poor, they may demand anything they wish—including a state with which to terrorize Israel.

It might seem that President Bush is being hypocritical: forbidding an ally, Israel, from fighting terrorism effectively even as U.S. forces wage a "war on terror." But observe that in fact he is being devastatingly consistent. For Bush, Iraqis are entitled to the sanctity of their Mosques—but our troops are forbidden from rooting out insurgents hiding and sniping from within; Iraqis are entitled to textbooks, hospitals, sewers, roads—but, in defending themselves, our troops must place the lives of Iraqi civilians (some of whom are or aid insurgents) above their own. Attesting to the cost of this sacrificial policy is the burgeoning U.S. death toll.

And Washington has refused to impose on Iraq a constitution

that would make the new regime non-threatening—as we did in Japan after World War II. In the name of satisfying the poor Iraqis' demand for "self-determination," President Bush has pledged to recognize as sovereign whatever regime the Iraqis vote for—even a militantly hostile Islamic theocracy that, in unison with Iran's mullahs, clamors for "Death to America."

Neither Israel nor the United States can vanquish Islamist terrorism unless it repudiates the corrupt morality of altruism, which enjoins the sacrifice of the successful as an ideal. Victory can only be achieved if one is convinced of one's moral right to live and to act consistently to achieve one's goals. Every self-effacing step that Israel takes—in lockstep with America and with our blessing—encourages the terrorists with the belief that their success is achievable.

The Advent of Freedom?

Onkar Ghate October 12, 2005

As the world eagerly watches the Iraqi constitutional referendum, the Bush administration and its intellectual supporters herald the occasion as a historic step toward freedom in the Middle East and security for America. This view betrays an appalling ignorance of the nature of freedom and the requirements of our national self-interest.

Politically, as America's Founding Fathers understood, to be free is to possess the ability to exercise one's rights to life, liberty, property and the pursuit of happiness. To be free means that no other men, whatever their number or position, can coercively prevent an individual from taking the steps rationally required to support his life. It means no one can force him to accept beliefs or dogmas, control what he can or cannot say, seize the material wealth he has produced and earned, or dictate the goals he must live for.

A constitution is valuable only if it strictly delimits the power of government to that of protecting each individual's rights. History demonstrates that government is, potentially, the worst violator of man's rights. A proper constitution declares off-limits any governmental action that would trespass on an individual's rights, no matter whether that action is proposed in the name of the king, the common good, God or public morality.

The draft Iraqi constitution, however, grants virtually unlimited power to the state.

As liberals have demanded in America for over a century, private property will be eviscerated. Although the proposed constitution nominally protects property rights, it explicitly allows that private property can be seized by the government "for the public interest." By contrast, public property "is sacrosanct, and its protection is the duty of every citizen." (In practice, this means that if the government takes a citizen's money, business or home, he must stand aside—and then defend with his life what the government has stolen from him.) The state will dictate whether an Iraqi can sell land to foreigners. It will manage the oil. It will provide to its hapless citizens "free" education and health care, "a correct environmental atmosphere," and work

---

This article originally appeared in *Capitalism Magazine*.

"that guarantees them a good life."

The government will also, as conservatives have long dreamed for America, enforce religious morality. "Islam," Article 2 declares, "is the official religion of the state and is a basic source of legislation: No law can be passed that contradicts the undisputed rules of Islam." Experts in Islamic law will sit on the Supreme Court. The state will guarantee protection of motherhood and the "ethical and religious value" of the family. Citizens will have freedom of speech, of press, of assembly—so long as no one says or does anything that violates "public morality," i.e., the dogmas of Islam.

And as if to leave no doubt that the state can exert total control over the individual's life, Article 45 adds that the government can restrict or limit "any of the freedoms and liberties stated in the constitution . . . as long as this restriction or limitation does not undermine the essence of the right or freedom." Of course, part of the essence of any right or freedom is that it is inviolable.

We in America had no reason to expect freedom from the drafters of Iraq's constitution. Like many of our own intellectuals on the left and the right (some of whom were advisers in Iraq), Iraqi intellectuals are either tribal or religious collectivists (or both). Whichever the case, they deny the individual and his rights. The tribalists deny material independence to the individual and seek to control his every economic step. The religionists, more numerous and powerful, deny spiritual independence to the individual and seek to dictate his every conviction and purpose in life. It is no accident that the draft constitution is both "keen to advance Iraqi tribes and clans" and eager to promote Islam. Freedom's intellectual preconditions do not exist in Iraq.

In the long term, whether Iraq's religious collectivists seize the machinery of state by a protracted, bloody civil war or by the ballot box will make no difference to America's security.

Nor did we have any reason to think that our self-defense requires, at the price of our soldiers' lives, "imposing freedom" on Iraq or the Middle East. It is true that free nations pose no threat to us. But neither do semi-barbarous nations when they and their citizens are demoralized—when they know that taking up arms against us guarantees their devastation. This is the lesson America's military should have taught the Islamic totalitarians and their legions of collectivist supporters and sympathizers in the Middle East after 9/11—indeed, after Iran's embassy takeover in 1979. But this is not the lesson conveyed by Operation Iraqi Freedom, which espouses Bush's "calling of our time": selflessly to bring freedom to those hostile to the idea.

Freedom is an intellectual achievement, which requires disavowal of collectivism and embrace of individualism. Sadly, no matter what the referendum's result, this is not what we are witnessing in Iraq.

Death to "Diplomacy" with Iran

Elan Journo   October 27, 2005

The president of Iran—a country believed to be building nuclear weapons—recently demanded that "Israel must be wiped off the map." But European diplomats, who are courting Iran in an attempt to halt its suspected nuclear weapons program, said that such belligerence won't derail their overtures.

The diplomatic effort led by Britain, France and Germany is touted as a reasonable way to settle the dispute over Iran's suspected nuclear weapons program without any losers. By enticing Iran to the negotiating table, we are told, the West can avoid a military confrontation, while Iran gains "economic incentives" that can help build its economy. But this deal—backed also by the Bush administration—can only strengthen Iran and turn it into a greater menace.

The European deal—which is said to include the sale of civilian aircraft and membership for Iran in the World Trade Organization—rests on the notion that no one would put abstract goals or principles ahead of gaining a steady flow of economic loot. And so, if only we could negotiate a deal that gives Iran a sufficiently juicy carrot, it would forgo its ambitions.

But to believe that Iran really hungers for nuclear energy (as it claims) is sheer fantasy. Possessing abundant oil and gas reserves, Iran is the second-largest oil producer in OPEC. To believe that it values prosperity at all is equally fantastic; Iran is a theocracy that systematically violates its citizens' right to political and economic liberty.

What Iran desires is a nuclear weapon—the better to threaten and annihilate the impious in the West and in Iran's neighborhood. Iran declares its anti-Western ambitions stridently. At an official parade in 2004, Iran flaunted a missile draped with a banner declaring: "We will crush America under our feet." (Its leaders, moreover, have for years repeated the demand that "Israel must be wiped off the map.")

A committed enemy of the West, Iran is the ideological wellspring of Islamic terrorism, and the "world's most active sponsor of terrorism" (according to the U.S. government). A totalitarian regime that viciously punishes "un-Islamic" behavior among its own citizens, Iran actively exports its contempt for freedom and human life throughout the infidel world. For years it has been fomenting and underwriting

savage attacks on Western and American interests, using such proxies as Hezbollah. Like several of the 9/11 hijackers before them, many
senior al-Qaeda leaders, fugitives of the Afghanistan war, have found
refuge in Iran. And lately Iran has funneled millions of dollars, arms
and ammunition to insurgents in Iraq.

It's absurd to think that by offering Iran rewards to halt its aggression, we will deflect it from its goal.

The only consequence of engaging such a vociferously hostile regime in negotiations is the whitewashing of its crimes and the granting of undeserved legitimacy. The attempt to conciliate Iran with "incentives" further inflames the boldness of Iran's mullahs. What it
teaches them is that the West lacks the intellectual self-confidence to
name its enemies and deal with them accordingly. It vindicates the
mullahs' view that their religious worldview can bring a scientific,
technologically advanced West to its knees.

Far from converting Iran into a non-threat, the "incentives"
would sustain its economy, prop up its dictatorial government and
perpetuate its terrorist war against the West. Whether Iran accepts the
European deal or merely prolongs "negotiations" indefinitely, so long
as the "diplomatic" approach continues Iran gains time enough to engage in covert nuclear-weapons research. Iran's flouting of a previous
agreement to stop enriching uranium (which prompted the current
talks) and its documented attempts to acquire nuclear-bomb technology erase any doubts about how it will behave under any future deal.

This approach of diplomacy-with-anyone-at-any-cost necessarily results in nourishing one's enemy and sharpening its fangs. That is
what happened under a 1994 deal with communist North Korea. In
return for boatloads of aid and oil from the United States, Japan and
other nations, North Korea promised not to develop nuclear weapons. Despite U.N. inspections, North Korea flouted the agreement repeatedly. When caught cheating, it promised anew to end its nuclear program in return for more "incentives." In February 2005, North
Korea declared (plausibly) that it had succeeded in building nuclear
weapons.

Another, older attempt to buy peace by giving "incentives" to
an enemy was a cataclysmic failure. In 1938 the Europeans pretended that Hitler's intentions were not really hostile, and insisted that
"peace in our time" could be attained by allowing him to walk into
Czechoslovakia. Instead, he was emboldened to launch World War II.

Ignoring the lessons of history, the Europeans are advocating a deal with Iran that likewise purchases the reckless pretense of peace today, at the cost of unleashing catastrophic dangers tomorrow.

To protect American (and European) lives, we must learn the life-or-death importance of passing objective moral judgment. We must recognize the character of Iran and act accordingly. By any rational standard, Iran should be condemned and its nuclear ambition thwarted, now. The brazenly amoral European gambit can only aid its quest—and necessitate a future confrontation with a bolder, stronger Iran.

The Twilight of Freedom of Speech

Onkar Ghate   February 21, 2006

To fathom our government's contemptible treatment of a handful of unbowed journalists, you must see the roots of that treatment in the moral ideal Christianity bequeathed the West.

In the face of the intimidation and murder of European authors, filmmakers and politicians by Islamic militants, a few European newspapers have the courage to defend their freedom of speech: they publish twelve cartoons to test whether it's still possible to criticize Islam. They discover it isn't. Muslims riot, burn embassies, and demand the censorship and death of infidels. The Danish cartoonists go into hiding; if they weren't afraid to speak before, they are now.

How do our leaders respond? Do they declare that an individual's freedom of speech is inviolable, no matter who screams offense at his ideas? No. Do they defend our right to life and pledge to hunt down anyone, anywhere, who abets the murder of a Westerner for having had the effrontery to speak? No—as they did not when the fatwah against Rushdie was issued or his translators were attacked and one murdered.

Instead, the U.S. government announces that although free speech is important, the government shares "the offense that Muslims have taken at these images," and even hints that it is disrespectful to publish them.

Why does a Muslim have a moral right to his dogmas, but we don't to our rational principles? Why, when journalists uphold free speech and Muslims respond with death threats, does the State Department single out the journalists for moral censure? Why the vicious double standard? Why admonish the good to mollify evil?

The answer lies in the West's conception of morality.

Morality, we are told incessantly, by secularists and religionists, the left and the right, means sacrifice; give up your values in selfless service to others. "Serve in a cause larger than your wants, larger than yourself," Bush proclaims to a believing nation.

But when you surrender your values, are you to give them up for men you admire, for those you think have earned and deserve them? Obviously not—otherwise yours would be an act of trade, of justice, of self-assertiveness, not self-sacrifice.

You must give to that which you don't admire, to that which you judge to be unworthy, undeserving, irrational. An employee, for instance, must give up his job for a competitor he deems inferior; a businessman must contribute to ideological causes he opposes; a taxpayer must fund modern, unemployed "artists" whose feces-covered works he loathes; the United States must finance the UN, which it knows to be a pack of America-hating dictatorships.

To uphold your rational convictions is the most selfish of acts. To renounce them, to surrender the world to that which you judge to be irrational and evil, is the epitome of sacrifice. When Jesus, the great preacher of self-sacrifice, commanded "Love your enemies, bless them that curse you, do good to them that hate you, and pray for them which despitefully use you, and persecute you," he knew whereof he spoke.

In the left's adaptation of this perverse ideal, selfless surrender to evil translates into a foreign policy of self-loathing and "sensitivity," of spitting in America and the West's face while showing respect for the barbarisms of every gang.

Bill Clinton, for instance, certainly no radical leftist, jumped into the recent fray to castigate us: "None of us are totally free of stereotypes about people of different races, different ethnic groups, and different religions . . . there was this appalling example in . . . Denmark . . . these totally outrageous cartoons against Islam."

In the right's version, selfless surrender to evil translates into a foreign policy of self-effacing service.

Our duty, Bush declares, is to bring the vote to Iraqis and Palestinians, but we dare not tell them what constitution to adopt, or ban the killers they want to vote for. We have no right to assert our principles, because they are rational and good. But the Iraqis and Palestinians have a right to enact their tribal and terrorist beliefs at our expense, because their beliefs are irrational and evil. In the present crisis, the State Department will not defend free speech, because this principle is rationally defensible; to unequivocally assert this value would be selfish. But the department will suggest that we respectfully refrain from publishing cartoons that upset the mental lethargy of self-made slaves to authority; Muslims have a right to their mystical taboos, precisely because the beliefs are mystical.

Tonight, when you turn on the news and see hatred-seething hordes burning the West's flags and torching its embassies, remember that this is the enemy your morality commands you to love and serve—and remember the lonely Danes hiding in fear for their lives. And then, in the ultimate act of self-assertiveness, pledge to renounce the morality of sacrifice and learn its opposite: the morality of rational self-interest. Though the West's twilight has begun, the darkness of suicide has not yet engulfed us. We still have a chance.

Washington's Failed War in Afghanistan

Elan Journo June 8, 2006

America's campaign in Afghanistan was once widely hailed as a success in the "war on terror." We have nothing more to fear from Afghanistan, our policy makers told us, because the war had accomplished its two main goals: al-Qaeda and its sponsoring regime, the Taliban, were supposedly long gone, and a new, pro-Western government had been set up. But as the daily news from Afghanistan shows, in reality the war has been a drastic failure.

Legions of undefeated Taliban and al-Qaeda soldiers have renewed their jihad. Flush with money, amassing recruits, and armed with guns, rockets and explosives, they are fighting to regain power. In recent months, they have mounted a string of deadly suicide bombings and rocket attacks against American and NATO forces; more U.S. troops have died in Afghanistan in the last twenty months than did during the peak of the war.

Taliban forces have effectively besieged several provinces in southern Afghanistan. Local officials estimate that in some provinces the "number of Taliban . . . is several times more than that of the police and Afghan National Army." Taliban fighters are said to amble through villages fearlessly, brandishing their Kalashnikovs, and collecting zakat (an Islamic tithe) from peasants. With astounding boldness, they have assassinated clerics and judges deemed too friendly to the new government, and fired rockets at a school for using "un-Islamic" books.

The Taliban and al-Qaeda forces are so strong and popular that Senator Bill Frist recently declared that a war against them cannot be won, and instead suggested negotiating with the Islamists.

How is it that five years after the war began—and in the face of America's unsurpassed military strength—Taliban and al-Qaeda fighters are threatening to regain power?

Victory in Afghanistan demanded two things. We had to destroy the Taliban and we had to ensure that a non-threatening, non-Islamic-warrior-breeding regime take its place. But we did not think we had a moral right to do what was necessary to achieve either goal.

Our military was ordered to pursue Taliban fighters only if it simultaneously showed "compassion" to the Afghans. The U.S. military dropped bombs on Afghanistan—but instead of ruthlessly pounding key targets, it was ordered to gingerly avoid hitting holy shrines and mosques (known to be Taliban hideouts) and to shower the country with food packages. The United States deployed ground forces—but instead of focusing exclusively on capturing or killing the enemy, they were also diverted to a host of "reconstruction" projects. The result is that the enemy was not destroyed and crushed in spirit, but merely scattered and left with the moral fortitude to regroup and launch a brazen comeback.

Even with its hands tied, however, the U.S. military succeeded in toppling the Taliban regime—but Washington subverted that achievement, too.

A new Afghan government would be a non-threat to America's interests if it were based on a secular constitution that respects individual rights. The Bush administration, however, declared that we had no right to "impose our beliefs" on the Afghans—and instead endorsed their desire for another regime founded on Islamic law. Already this avowedly Islamic regime has jailed an Afghan magazine editor for "blasphemy"; earlier this year Abdul Rahman, an Afghan convert to Christianity, faced a death sentence for apostasy. The new Afghan regime cannot be counted on to oppose the resurgence of Islamic totalitarianism. Ideologically, it has nothing to say in opposition to the doctrines of the Taliban (two members of the Taliban leadership are in the new government). It is only a matter of time before Afghanistan is once again a haven for anti-American warriors.

The failure in Afghanistan is a result of Washington's foreign policy. Despite lip-service to the goal of protecting America's safety, the "war on terror" has been waged in compliance with the prevailing moral premise that self-interest is evil and self-sacrifice a virtue. Instead of trouncing the enemy for the sake of protecting American lives, our leaders have sacrificed our self-defense for the sake of serving the whims of Afghans.

The half-hearted war in Afghanistan failed to smash the Taliban and al-Qaeda. It failed to render their ideology—Islamic totalitarianism—a lost cause. Instead, at best it demonstrated Washington's reluctance to fight ruthlessly to defend Americans. How better to stoke the enthusiasm of jihadists?

America cannot win this or any war by embracing selflessness as a virtue. Ultimately, it cannot survive unless Washington abandons its self-sacrificial foreign policy in favor of one that proudly places America's interests as its exclusive moral concern.

The U.S.-Israeli Suicide Pact

Elan Journo July 20, 2006

The Iran-Hamas-Hezbollah axis is fully responsible for initiating the war on Israel, but the Islamists' aggression is the logical product of U.S.-Israeli policy. The longstanding commitment of Israel and America to "diplomatic engagement" with Palestinians and Islamists—a euphemism for appeasement—is suicidal.

For decades America has urged Israel to placate and surrender to our common enemy. The U.S.-endorsed "Road Map to Peace," like the "Peace Process" and sundry initiatives before it, rationalized Palestinian terrorism as the result of a legitimate grievance. If only the Palestinians' wish for a civilized, peaceful state were fulfilled—Washington deluded itself into believing—terrorism would end. And fulfilling this wish requires not smashing their terrorist infrastructure, but showering them with land and loot.

But the majority of Palestinians actually seek the destruction of Israel, and the slaughter of its people. Because they embrace this vicious goal, hordes of Palestinians idolized arch terrorist Yasser Arafat for waging a terrorist war to wipe out Israel and establish a nationalist dictatorship. They abetted Arafat's terrorism and celebrated his atrocities. They served as cheerleaders or recruits for terrorist groups—and when they had the chance, they embraced the even more militant religious zealots of Hamas. It is no surprise that, according to a recent poll, 77 percent of Palestinians support their government's kidnapping of an Israeli soldier and that 60 percent support the continued rocket fire from Gaza into Israel.

But even as Palestinians mounted more attacks, Washington pressed Israel for more concessions—and bolstered the terrorist-sponsoring Palestinian Authority with millions of dollars in aid. The U.S. forbade Israel from laying a finger on Arafat, and extended this tender solicitude to Hamas leaders. Washington actually whitewashed the blood-stained Arafat and his crony Mahmoud Abbas as peace-loving statesmen and invited them to the White House. And when Hezbollah now fires rockets at major cities in northern Israel, President Bush demands that Israel show "restraint."

Depressingly, Israel has continually relented to American pressure to appease our common enemy. It has prostrated itself before the Palestinians, with flamboyantly self-sacrificial offers of land-for-peace; it has withdrawn from southern Lebanon, ceding ground necessary to its self-defense; it has withdrawn from Gaza, leaving its southern cities at the mercy of rocket fire from the Hamas-run territory.

Such U.S.-endorsed appeasement by Israel, across decades, has enabled Hezbollah and Hamas to mount their current attacks. Yet America remains undeterred in its commitment to appeasement.

The U.S. is now trying to woo Iran with endless offers of economic "incentives," if only Iran promises to stop chasing nuclear weapons. Evading Iran's lust to "wipe Israel off the map," evading its funding of Hezbollah and Hamas, evading its avowed enmity to America, evading its decades of fomenting and orchestrating a proxy terror war against American civilians—evading all of this, Washington deludes itself into believing that paying Iran off will, somehow, wipe out its hostility.

Inevitably, this encourages Iran to continue its aggressive support for terrorists and its fervent quest for nuclear weapons. Merely by prolonging the negotiations endlessly, Iran gains time to acquire a weapon to wield against its neighbors, to provide to Hamas and Hezbollah or to other proxies to use against the United States. And were Iran eventually to accept some deal, American aid would merely be sustaining Iran's regime—and, inexorably, a covert nuclear program.

We are teaching the Islamic totalitarians in Gaza, Lebanon and Iran that their goal of destroying us is legitimate; that aggression is practical; that the more aggressive they are, the more we will surrender. U.S.-Israeli policy has demonstrated that we lack the intellectual self-confidence to name, let alone condemn, our enemies—and that we lack the will to deal with threats mercilessly. It vindicates the Islamists' premise that their religious worldview can bring a scientific, technologically advanced West to its knees.

To protect the lives of our citizens, America and Israel must stop evading the nature of the enemy's cause: our complete destruction. We must stop appeasing our common enemy—and embrace self-defense as a matter of intransigent principle. To put an end to the current rocket attacks from Lebanon and Gaza, America should urge Israel to annihilate the annihilators: Hamas and Hezbollah. And to thwart Iran's nuclear ambition, America must use as much military force as is necessary to dispose of that catastrophic threat and the regime responsible for it.

The Indispensable Condition of Peace

Onkar Ghate July 21, 2006

As Israeli soldiers reenter Gaza and bomb Lebanon, and Israeli citizens seek shelter from Hezbollah's missiles, the world despairingly wonders whether peace between Israel and its neighbors can ever take root. It can—but only if America reverses course.

To achieve peace in the Middle East, as in any region, there is a necessary principle that every party must learn: the initiation of force is evil. And the indispensable means of teaching it is to ensure that the initiating side is defeated and punished. Decisive retaliatory force must be wielded against the aggressor. So long as one side has reason to think it will benefit from initiating force against its neighbors, war must result. Yet this is precisely what America's immoral foreign policy gives the Palestinian Authority, Hamas and Hezbollah reason to think.

Israel is a free country, which recognizes the rights of its citizens, whatever their race or religion, and which prospers through business and trade. It has no use for war and no interest in conquest. But for years, Arafat and the Palestinian authorities, with the aid of Iran, Syria, Saudi Arabia and other states, sought not to learn the conditions of freedom, but to annihilate the only free nation in their midst: Israel. Did the United States demand that the Palestinian leadership be destroyed?

No. Clinton invited Arafat to dine at the White House and Bush declared that peace requires Israel to give in to its aggressor's insistence on a state.

Worse still, as part of the "two state solution" announced in 2002, Bush demanded that Israel withdraw to its pre-1967 borders. In 1967 Israel captured the Golan Heights, West Bank and Gaza Strip after yet another attempt by Arab nations to annihilate it. To give back any of this land—as Israel has done in the face of international pressure—teaches the Arabs that they can launch wars against Israel with impunity. If they at first do not succeed militarily, they need only continue issuing threats against Israel and arming more suicide bombers—and eventually the land they lost in a war they initiated will be returned to them. They can then start the process anew, as they have since Israel

---

This article originally appeared in *Ynetnews.com*.

withdrew from Lebanon and Gaza.

In order to move toward his "two state solution," Bush championed elections in the Palestinian territories and Lebanon, which predictably brought Hamas and Hezbollah into government. Terrorism, Bush is thus teaching the killers, is the means to political power.

The reason peace eludes the Middle East is therefore not difficult to discern. The lesson President Bush is conveying to the Arabs and Islamists—that the initiation of force is practical—is a continuation of the lesson America's foreign policy has been teaching them for decades. The Egyptians seized the Suez canal from the French and British in 1956—and we demanded that the Europeans not retaliate. Israel had the Palestinian terrorists surrounded in Lebanon in 1982—and we brokered their release. Many Arabs idolized a terrorist for hijacking airliners and murdering civilians—and we poured money into his regime, hailed him for winning the Nobel Peace Prize in 1994, and demanded that Israel enter into a protracted "peace process" that consisted of concession after concession. What possible conclusion could the Arab world draw but that the initiation of force is practical? So long as they have grounds to believe that, war is inescapable.

If we truly seek peace, we must reverse this perverse lesson. We must proclaim the objective conditions of peace. This means declaring to Arab nations that Israel, as a free country, has a moral right to exist, that the Arabs and Palestinians are the initiators of the conflict and that aggression on their part is evil and will not be tolerated. And it means encouraging Israel not to negotiate and compromise with its current assailants, but to destroy them.

Only when the initiators of force learn that their actions lead not to world sympathy and political power, but to their own deaths, will peace be possible in the Middle East.

Why We Are Losing Hearts and Minds

Keith Lockitch September 7, 2006

Five years into our "war on terror," the Iraqi insurgency is raging, with no apparent end to the new recruits eager to wage jihad against the West. Support for offensive action has faded among a disheartened American public, while the terrorists are growing in number and in boldness.

Where have our leaders gone wrong? What kind of leadership failure can demoralize a whole nation of honest, productive citizens, while leaving suicide murderers stirred to righteous action?

The power that inspires righteous action—and which, by its absence, breeds discouragement—is the power of moral idealism. What has brought us to our present state is our leaders' moral weakness in response to the jihadists' moral zeal.

Observe that what draws the recruits to terrorist cells is a powerful ideal: the advancement of their religion. The jihadists believe fervently that Islam is the revealed word of Allah, that selfless submission to Allah is the purpose of life, and that all individuals should be subjugated to Islamic law under a theocracy. They believe in spreading the rule of Islam worldwide and killing any "infidels" who stand in their way. They are morally outraged by the American ideal of individual liberty and regard our this-worldly, capitalistic culture as an evil that must be destroyed.

America can only defend itself against such a zealous, militant movement if we have moral confidence in our own ideals—and fight for them. We must repudiate the Islamists' "ideals" of other-worldliness, of blind faith, of renunciation and suffering, of theocracy, and proudly uphold the superior, American ideals of reason, freedom and the pursuit of worldly happiness.

But our leaders have not shown such moral confidence.

When the terrorists of September 11 struck in the name of Islam, President Bush did not identify them as Islamic totalitarians and condemn their murderous ideology and its supporters. Instead, he painted the hijackers as a band of isolated lunatics who had "hijacked a great religion." (Only recently has President Bush even acknowledged that our enemy is Islamic, with his use of the term "Islamic fascism.")

In response to Muslim denunciations of America's secularism, our leaders did not defend this attribute of America, but instead stressed Americans' religiosity. A mere two weeks after September 11, with the ruins of the World Trade Towers still smoldering, our planned Afghanistan campaign, "Operation Infinite Justice," was renamed to appease Muslims protesting that only Allah can dispense "infinite justice."

Unable to defend America intellectually, our leaders are unable to defend her militarily.

Have our leaders acted consistently against terrorist regimes? Consider our policy toward Iran, the primary state sponsor of terrorism. Refusing to identify Iran as the fatherland of Islamic totalitarianism, our president initially beseeched its mullahs to join our "war on terror." And he has consistently answered their chants of "Death to America" and their quest for nuclear weapons with negotiation and spineless diplomacy.

Have our leaders asserted that they will use America's formidable military to secure our way of life by whatever means necessary? No. Lacking the moral confidence to defeat our enemies, they have instead squandered our military resources and sacrificed our brave soldiers in a futile quest to spread "democracy" around the globe—as though bringing the vote to Muslim mobs sympathetic to Islamic totalitarianism will somehow end the terrorist threat.

The reason the terrorists and their state sponsors are not demoralized is that our leaders have failed to demoralize them. Our leaders' words and actions have signaled that we are not as morally committed to our lives and freedom as the terrorists are to our destruction.

We must make it clear to the jihadists that we will destroy anyone who takes up arms for Islamic totalitarianism. No one wants to fight and die for a hopeless cause. The jihadists will continue to be emboldened and to attract new recruits until they are convinced their goal is unachievable. They must see that we have the moral confidence to defend our lives—to answer their violence with an overwhelming military response, without pulling punches. They must see us willing to visit such crushing devastation on them that they fear us more than they fear Allah.

It is often said that we must win the "hearts and minds" of supporters of totalitarian Islam. Indeed we must: their hearts must be made to despair at the futility of their cause, and their minds must be convinced that any threat to our lives and freedom will bring them swift and certain doom.

The ideologues of totalitarian Islam have seized the power of moral idealism in the service of our destruction. It is time we reclaimed that power in defense of our freedom.

What Real War Looks Like

Elan Journo December 7, 2006

The Iraq Study Group has issued many specific recommendations, but the options boil down to a maddeningly limited range: pull out or send more troops to do democracy-building and, either way, "engage" the hostile regimes in Iran and Syria. Missing from the list is the one option our self-defense demands: a war to defeat the enemy. If you think we've already tried this option and failed, think again. Washington's campaign in Iraq looks nothing like the war necessary for our self-defense.

What does such a war look like?

America's security depends on identifying precisely the enemy that threatens our lives—and then crushing it, rendering it a non-threat. It depends on proudly defending our right to live free of foreign aggression—by unapologetically killing the killers who want us dead.

Those who say this is a "new kind of conflict" against a "faceless enemy" are wrong. The enemy Washington evasively calls "terrorism" is actually an ideologically inspired political movement: Islamic totalitarianism. It seeks to subjugate the West under a totalitarian Islamic regime by means of terrorism, negotiation, war—anything that will win its jihad. The movement's inspiration, its first triumph, its standard bearer, is the theocracy of Iran. Iran's regime has, for decades, used terrorist proxies to attack America. It openly seeks nuclear weapons and zealously sponsors and harbors jihadists. Without Iran's support, legions of holy warriors would be untrained, unarmed, unmotivated, impotent.

Destroying Islamic totalitarianism requires a punishing military onslaught to end its primary state representative (Iran) and demoralize its supporters. We need to deploy all necessary force to destroy Iran's ability to fight, while minimizing our own casualties. We need a campaign that ruthlessly inflicts the pain of war so intensely that the jihadists renounce their cause as hopeless and fear to take up arms against us. This is how America and its Allies defeated both Nazi Germany and Imperialist Japan.

Victory in World War II required flattening cities, firebombing factories, shops and homes, devastating vast tracts of Germany and Japan. The enemy and its supporters were exhausted materially and crushed in spirit. What our actions demonstrated to them was that any attempt to implement their vicious ideologies would bring them only destruction and death. Since their defeat, Nazism and Japanese imperialism have essentially withered as ideological forces. Victory today requires the same: smashing Iran's totalitarian regime and thus demoralizing the Islamist movement and its many supporters, so that they, too, abandon their cause as futile.

We triumphed over both Japan and Germany in less than four years after Pearl Harbor. Yet more than five years after 9/11, against a far weaker enemy, our soldiers still die daily in Iraq. Why? Because this war is neither assertive nor ruthless—it is a tragically meek pretense at war.

Consider what Washington has done. The Islamist regime in Iran remains untouched, fomenting terrorism. (And now our leaders hope to "engage" Iran diplomatically.)

We went to battle not with theocratic Iran, but with the secular dictatorship of Iraq. And the campaign there was not aimed at crushing whatever threat Hussein's regime posed to us. "Shock and awe" bombing never materialized. Our brave and capable forces were hamstrung: ordered not to bomb key targets such as power plants and to avoid firing into mosques (where insurgents hide) lest we offend Muslim sensibilities. Instead, we sent our troops to lift Iraq out of poverty, open new schools, fix up hospitals, feed the hungry, unclog sewers—a Peace Corps, not an army corps, mission.

U.S. troops were sent, not to crush an enemy threatening America, but (as Bush explained) to "sacrifice for the liberty of strangers," putting the lives of Iraqis above their own. They were prevented from using all necessary force to win or even to protect themselves. No wonder the insurgency has flourished, emboldened by Washington's self-crippling policies. (Perversely, some want even more Americans tossed into this quagmire.)

Bush did all this to bring Iraqis the vote. Any objective assessment of the Middle East would have told one who would win elections, given the widespread popular support for Islamic totalitarianism. Iraqis swept to power a pro-Islamist leadership intimately tied to Iran. The most influential figure in Iraqi politics is now Moktadr al-Sadr, an Islamist warlord lusting after theocratic rule and American blood. When asked whether he would accept just such an outcome from the elections, Bush said that of course he would, because "democracy is democracy."

No war that ushers Islamists into political office has U.S. self-defense as its goal.

This war has been worse than doing nothing, because it has galvanized our enemy to believe its success more likely than ever—even as it has drained Americans' will to fight. Washington's feeble campaign demonstrates the ruinous effects of refusing to assert our self-interest and defend our freedom. It is past time to consider our only moral and practical option: end the senseless sacrifice of our soldiers—and let them go to war.

The Real Disgrace:
Washington's Battlefield "Ethics"

Elan Journo July 3, 2007

Americans rightly admire our troops for their bravery, dedication and integrity. The Marines, for instance, are renowned for abiding by an honorable code—as warriors and as individuals in civilian life. They epitomize the rectitude of America's soldiers. But a recently disclosed Pentagon study—little noted in the media—has seemingly cast a shadow over our troops.

The study of U.S. combat troops in Iraq finds that less than half of the soldiers and Marines surveyed would report a team member for breaches of the military's ethics rules. Military and civilian observers have concluded from the study that more and stricter training in combat ethics is urgently needed.

But instead of reinforcing the military's ethics, we must challenge them. The Pentagon study provides evidence for a searing indictment not of our soldiers but of Washington's rules of engagement.

Consider the waking nightmare of being a U.S. combat soldier in Iraq: imagine that you are thrust into a battlefield—but purposely hamstrung by absurd restrictions. Iraqis throw Molotov cocktails (i.e., gasoline-filled bottles) at your vehicle—but you are prohibited from responding by force. Iraqis, to quote the study, "drop large chunks of concrete blocks from second story buildings or overpasses" as you drive by—but you are not allowed to respond. "Every group of Soldiers and Marines interviewed," the Pentagon study summarizes, "reported that they felt the existing ROE [rules of engagement] tied their hands, preventing them from doing what needed to be done to win the war."

And the soldiers are right. In Iraq Washington's rules have systematically prevented our brave and capable troops from using all necessary force to win, to crush the insurgency—and even to protect themselves. As noted in news articles since the start of the war, American forces are ordered not to bomb key targets such as power plants, and to avoid firing into mosques (where insurgents hide) lest they offend Muslim sensibilities.

This article originally appeared in *FrontPageMagazine.com*.

Having to follow such self-effacing rules of engagement while confronting sniper fire and ambushes and bombs from every direction, day in and day out, must be utterly demoralizing and unbearable. No one should be surprised at the newly reported willingness of combat troops to defy military ethics, because such defiance is understandable as the natural reaction of warriors made to follow suicidal rules.

When being "ethical" on Washington's terms means martyring yourself and your comrades for the sake of murderous Iraqis, it is understandable that troops are disinclined to report "unethical" behavior. It is understandable that troops should feel anger and anxiety (as many do), because it is horrifically unjust for America to send its personnel into combat, deliberately prevent them from achieving victory—and expect them to die for the sake of the enemy. It would be natural for an individual thrust into the line of fire as a sacrificial offering to rebel with indignation at such a fate.

How can we do this to our soldiers?

The death and misery caused by Washington's self-crippling rules of engagement—rules endorsed by liberals and conservatives alike—are part of the inevitable destruction flowing from a broader evil: the philosophy of "compassionate" war.

This perverse view of war holds that fighting selfishly to defend your own freedom by defeating enemies is wrong; but fighting to selflessly serve the needs of others is virtuous. It was on this premise that U.S. troops were sent to Iraq: Washington's goal was not to defend America against whatever threat Hussein's hostile regime posed to us, as a first step toward defeating our enemies in the region—principally Iran, the arch sponsor of Islamic totalitarianism. Instead the troops were sent (as Bush explained) to "sacrifice for the liberty of strangers"—spilling American blood and spending endless resources on the "compassionate" goal of lifting the hostile and primitive Iraqi people out of poverty, feeding their hungry, unclogging their sewers. The result of this "compassionate" war is thousands of unnecessary American deaths, and the preservation and emboldening of the enemies we most need to defeat: Iran and Saudi Arabia.

We must put an end to the barbarous sacrifice of American troops, now. It is past time to abandon Washington's self-sacrificial rules of engagement, and its broader policy of "compassionate," self-sacrificial warfare. Instead of subjecting troops to more intensive "ethics" training, we should unleash them from the militarily suicidal ethics of self-sacrifice.

The Pakistan Crisis

Elan Journo   December 29, 2007

The assassination of Benazir Bhutto has, we're told, upended Washington's foreign policy. "Our foreign policy has relied on her presence as a stabilizing force. . . . Without her, we will have to re-group," explained Sen. Arlen Specter (R-Pa.) in the *Washington Post.* "It complicates life for the American government."

But in fact U.S. policy was in disarray long before the assassination.

U.S. diplomats have been scrambling for months to do something about the growing power of Islamists in the nuclear-armed nation which Washington hails as a "major non-NATO ally." Having supported President Musharraf's authoritarian regime, Washington helped broker the deal to allow Bhutto back into Pakistan, hoping she might create a pro-U.S. regime, but then decided to push Musharraf to share power with Bhutto, then insisted that he's "indispensable," but also flirted with the idea of backing Bhutto.

All this against the backdrop of the creeping Talibanization of Pakistan. Islamist fighters once "restricted to untamed mountain villages along the [Pakistani-Afghan] border," now "operate relatively freely in cities like Karachi," according to *Newsweek.* The Taliban "now pretty much come and go as they please inside Pakistan." They are easily slipping in and out of neighboring Afghanistan to arm and train their fighters, and foster attacks on the West.

Why has Washington proven so incapable of dealing with this danger to U.S. security? The answer lies in how we embraced Pakistan as an ally.

Pakistan was an improbable ally. In the 1990s its Inter-Services Intelligence agency had helped bring the Taliban to power; Gen. Musharraf's regime, which began in 1999, formally endorsed the Taliban regime; and many in Pakistan support the cause of jihad (taking to the streets to celebrate 9/11). But after 9/11 the Bush administration asserted that we needed Pakistan as an ally, and that the alternatives to Gen. Musharraf's military dictatorship were far worse.

If the administration was right about that (which is doubtful), we could have had an alliance with Pakistan under only one condition—treating this supposedly lesser of two evils as, indeed, evil.

It would have required acknowledging the immorality of

Pakistan's past and demanding that it vigorously combat the Islamic totalitarians as proof of repudiating them. Alert to the merest hint of Pakistan's disloyalty, we'd have had to keep the dictatorial regime at arm's length. This would have meant openly declaring that both the regime and the pro-jihadists among Pakistan' people are immoral, that our alliance is delimited to one goal, and that we would welcome and support new, pro-American leaders in Pakistan who actually embrace freedom.

But instead, Washington evaded Pakistan's pro-Islamist past and pretended that this corrupt regime was good. We offered leniency on Pakistan's billion-dollar debts, opened up a fire hose of financial aid, lifted economic sanctions, and blessed the regime simply because it agreed to call itself our ally and pay lip-service to enacting "reforms." After Musharraf pledged his "full support" and "unstinting cooperation," we treated the dictator as if he were some freedom-loving statesman, and effectively whitewashed the regime.

Since we did not demand any fundamental change in Pakistan's behavior as the price of our alliance, we should not have expected any.

Pakistan's "unstinting cooperation" included help with the token arrests of a handful of terrorists—even as the country became a haven for Islamists. Since 2001, Islamists have established a stronghold in the Pakistani-Afghan tribal borderlands (where bin Laden may be hiding). But our "ally" neither eradicated them nor allowed U.S. forces to do so. Instead in 2006, Musharraf reached a truce with them: in return for the Islamists' "promise" not to attack Pakistani soldiers, not to establish their own Taliban-like rule and not to support foreign jihadists—Pakistan backed off and released 165 captured jihadists.

Far from protesting, President Bush endorsed this appeasing deal, saying: "When [Musharraf] looks me in the eye and says" this deal will stop "the Talibanization of the people, and that there won't be a Taliban and won't be al-Qaeda, I believe him."

We have gone on paying Pakistan for its "cooperation," to the tune of $10 billion in aid. The Islamists, who predictably reneged on the truce, now have a new staging area in Pakistan from which to plot attacks on us (perhaps, one day, with Pakistani nukes).

Why did our leaders evade Pakistan's true nature? Faced with the need to do something against the totalitarian threat, it was far easier to pretend that Musharraf was a great ally who will help rid us of our problems if we would only uncritically embrace him. To declare Musharraf's regime evil, albeit the lesser of two evils, would have required a deep moral confidence in the righteousness of our cause. The Bush administration didn't display this confidence in our own fight against the Taliban, allowing the enablers of bin Laden to flee rather than ruthlessly destroying them. Why would it display such confidence in dealing with Pakistan?

But no matter how much one pretends that facts are not facts, eventually they will rear their heads.

This is why we are so unable to deal with the threat of Pakistan. Our blindness is self-induced.

POSTSCRIPT

What We Knew About Pakistan, Islamists and bin Laden

Elan Journo   March 26, 2014

Osama bin Laden spent nearly six tranquil years hidden in a com-pound in Abbottabad, Pakistan. Since that came to light in May 2011, the *New York Times*'s reporter Carlotta Gall has been chas-ing down leads to figure out what Pakistan knew about bin Laden. Gall's article vividly recounts the trail leading to the answer, but re-veals more than that.

First, the answer: her search culminates with an unnamed source admitting that the Pakistani intelligence agency, ISI, "actually ran a special desk assigned to handle bin Laden. It was operated inde-pendently, led by an officer who made his own decisions and did not report to a superior. He handled only one person: bin Laden." That may be the closest thing to a smoking gun that you might hope for, given the corruption and opacity of the Pakistani regime. Which brings us to the other revelation.

Pakistan's post-9/11 alliance with the United States was a massive fraud. Pakistan had declared itself "with us" but as Gall points out in-cidentally (echoing a view others have also expressed): "the strategy that has evolved in Pakistan has been to make a show of cooperation with the American fight against terrorism while covertly abetting and even coordinating Taliban, Kashmiri and foreign Qaeda-linked militants."

> The United States was neither speaking out against
> Pakistan nor changing its policy toward a government that
> was exporting terrorism, the [Pakistani] legislator lament-
> ed. "How many people have to die before they get it? They
> are standing by a military that protects, aids and abets peo-
> ple who are going against the U.S. and Western mission in
> Afghanistan, in Syria, everywhere."

As I argue in *Winning the Unwinnable War*, Washington was a willing enabler of the fraud. The U.S.-Pakistan relationship was predicated on an evasion of the Pakistani regime's character. After 9/11
the Bush administration wanted to believe that this corrupt regime,
which had backed the Taliban, could transform itself overnight in to
a good regime. So we treated it as if it already were. The U.S. uncritically blessed the regime, while Pakistan paid lip-service to the notion
of being allied with us. For the low, low price of $10 billion-plus, we
acquired a new "ally" who turned around and betrayed us, repeatedly.
(In the book, I describe some of Pakistan's overt betrayals.) We turned
a blind eye. And kept doing that. But wishing away facts is futile.

You might recall that the Bush administration was widely cri-
tiqued for being (of all things) "moralistic" in its foreign policy. So
much for that.

The Price of Bush's Commitment to Palestinian Statehood

Elan Journo   March 30, 2008

On his recent visit to the Middle East, Vice President Cheney voiced the Bush administration's belief that a Palestinian state is "long overdue" and vowed to help make that goal a reality. Many conservatives and liberals agree with the administration that America should help fulfill the long-deferred Palestinian aspirations to statehood. The idea is that in doing so we would go a long way toward dousing the flames of Islamist terrorism.

But does U.S. backing for Palestinian statehood advance our security?

Only if you think we're better off fostering a new terrorist state.

That may seem excessively harsh given President Bush's mantra that Palestinians just want "the opportunity to use [their talents and] gifts to better their own lives and build a future for their children." The Bush line we keep hearing is that the terrorists and their supporters are but a fringe element that will be marginalized under the new state, which will coexist "side by side in peace" with Israel and the Western world.

But listen to Palestinian clerics at Friday sermons, calling for violent attacks on Israel. Look at the lurid posters in the homes and shops of ordinary Palestinians, passionately glorifying "martyrs" and terrorist kingpins. Look at their coordinated digging of tunnels to smuggle in weapons and explosives. Look at the popular collusion with Islamist militants and their stream of recruits. Recall the years of ferocious attacks against Israeli towns.

If the mass of Palestinians just want peace and a better life, they would not despise and war against the only state in the region, Israel, that protects individual rights and that offers a standard of living far superior to (even the richest) Arab regimes. They would be far better off, freer and safer, if they put away their rocks, bullets and dynamite belts and sought to live and work in Israel (as some once did).

Instead, they flood the streets to protest negotiations about peaceful co-existence with Israel. Ideologically, their dominant factions are the Islamic totalitarians of Hamas and the nationalist terrorists of Fatah. These differ only in their form of dictatorship—religious or ethnic. Both promise their followers, one way or another, to wipe out Israel.

That hostility to Israel, the only free nation in the Middle East, should make any U.S. president stand firmly against the Palestinian cause. Particularly in a post-9/11 world, Washington should recognize that U.S. security is strengthened by preventing Islamist terrorists from securing another stronghold and training ground.

Given the overwhelming evidence that it would undermine U.S. security, what explains the Bush administration's come-hell-or-highwater promise to do "everything we can" to back a Palestinian state? It is the administration's belief that America has a duty to ease the suffering of the world's wretched, regardless of the cost in lives to us.

That's why, after Palestinians brought Hamas to power in a landslide, Washington responded with "compassion" for their "humanitarian" needs. Of course the U.S. and its European allies felt compelled to "isolate" the Hamas regime by cutting off direct aid to the Palestinian Authority. But they refused to believe the Palestinians themselves should be held responsible for how they voted, because they're already dirt poor. This meant suspending our judgment and absolving Palestinians of culpability for choosing murderers to lead them. So, despite the embargo on aid to the Hamas-led government, in 2006 U.S. aid to Palestinians increased by 17 percent to $468 million, propping up their terrorist proto-state.

This policy's result is to endorse, facilitate and vitalize Palestinian aggression. We've seen the unleashing of a popularly supported Hamas-Hezbollah war against Israel in 2006 and ongoing attacks springing from Gaza. Al-Qaeda has reportedly already set up shop alongside other jihadists in the Palestinian territories. Just imagine the mushrooming of terrorist training camps and explosives factories under a sovereign Palestinian state. Imagine how emboldened jihadists will feel operating under a regime that Washington has created and blessed.

This is the price of a policy based not on furthering U.S. security, but on undeserved pity. This is the price of willfully ignoring the vile nature of Palestinian goals, treating these hostile people as above reproach and rewarding their irrationality.

Isn't it time we demand a policy that puts our security first?

Bush's War Policy:
The Top Campaign Non-Issue?

Elan Journo June 12, 2008

It's staggering to think that as we march toward a seventh year at war, Iraq (let alone Afghanistan) is hardly an issue on the campaign trail. Of course, nobody has forgotten about the war. But there's been no substantive debate on it, either.

John McCain, echoing many conservatives, regularly touts the supposed gains of the "surge." Upon his return from visiting Iraq, he declared, "We're succeeding. I don't care what anybody says. I've seen the facts on the ground." Hillary Clinton and Barak Obama even grudgingly conceded, at one point, that the "surge" was working. And when they do challenge President Bush's war policy, they complain not about its goals, but about the crushing financial cost.

The war's a backburner issue in the campaign because—strange as it may sound—critics and cheerleaders of the president's policy judge it by the same spurious benchmark. They focus myopically on whether insurgents have been kicked out, for the time being, from one street, in some neighborhood of Baghdad. If that's success, then the issue can be pushed out of mind.

But nobody would have bought that as a vision of success, in the devastating aftermath of 9/11. And nobody should buy it now. The only rational benchmark for success is whether Washington's policies have made the lives of Americans safer from the threat of Islamists. Judged by that standard, Bush's war policy is an abject failure.

Bush vowed to "pursue nations that provide aid or safe haven to terrorism," and warned that either "you are with us, or you are with the terrorists." Bush's war policy, however, was not to target the greatest threat, but instead to minister to those in greatest need. It was to show compassion to oppressed Iraqis and Afghans, to raise them out of poverty, to give them elections.

Six-plus years into a "war on terror," Washington has done nothing to counter the spearhead of the global jihadist movement, the Islamic Republic of Iran. The United States has allowed it to grow stronger. Iran races to acquire nuclear weapons; it taunts and threatens our naval

---

This article originally appeared in *Capitalism Magazine*.

vessels; it arms and trains insurgents in Iraq in attacking Americans; it backs jihadists across the region—all with impunity.

What about Iraq? More than 4,000 U.S. troops died so that hostile Iraqis could elect a new gang of anti-Americans to sit in Baghdad's parliament. Iraq's government is still dominated by Islamist groups, which still operate death squads, and it is still deep, deep in Iran's pocket.

Across the Middle East, Washington campaigned for elections in the strongholds of various Islamist groups—such as Hamas and Hezbollah—that it should have worked to destroy. Many people, true to their ideological beliefs, voted to give these groups more political power. Naturally, the jihadists feel encouraged. According to a new study, the Iranian-backed Hamas has amassed at least eighty tons of explosives in Gaza since 2007, and it has also got its hands on anti-tank weapons. So expect another Islamist war emanating from the terrorist proto-state of "Hamas-stan," which Bush's policy helped create.

In Afghanistan and Pakistan, according to the U.S. National Intelligence Director, al-Qaeda is gaining in strength and prepping new recruits who can blend into American society and attack domestic targets. Jihadists are now fighting to reconquer Afghanistan, and to "Talibanize" large patches of Pakistan. The Afghan-Pakistan border, reports the National Intelligence Director, "serves as a staging area for al-Qaeda's attacks in support of the Taliban in Afghanistan as well as a location for training new terrorist operatives, for attacks in Pakistan, the Middle East, Africa, Europe and the United States."

This is what Bush's war policy has achieved: an enemy that has no fear of us, that spits in our face, and that is gearing up to kill more of us.

This is what a "compassionate" war policy, aimed not at defeating our enemies but at serving the welfare of Iraqis and Afghans, had to achieve. It is a policy that put their lack of freedom and lack of wealth, ahead of our moral right to end the threat of Islamist aggression. Bush's policy held that it was our duty to enable these hostile peoples to vote their political conscience—while evading the fact that so many avidly support jihadist goals.

Shame on Republicans for promising to stay the same disastrous course and toss thousands more troops onto the sacrificial pyre of Iraq. Shame on Democrats for squandering the opportunity of a campaign year to offer us a real Plan B—an alternative policy that would actually combat state sponsors of terrorism.

Each of us deserves—and should demand—more of our leaders. We deserve a foreign policy that truly upholds our right to security.

The Wreckage:
A Look Back at Bush's Democracy Crusade

Elan Journo Fall 2008

A Review of *Mugged by Reality: The Liberation of Iraq and the Failure of Good Intentions*, by John Agresto. New York: Encounter Books, 2007.

The measure of success in the Iraq war has undergone a curious progression. Early on, the Bush administration held up the vision of a peaceful, prosperous, pro-Western Iraq as its benchmark. But the torture chambers of Saddam Hussein were replaced by the horrors of a sadistic sectarian war and a fierce insurgency that consumed thousands of American lives. And the post-invasion Iraqi regime, it turns out, is led by Islamist parties allied with religious militias and intimately tied to the belligerent Iranian regime. The benchmark, if we can call it that, then shrank to the somewhat lesser vision of an Iraqi government that can stand up on its own, so that America can stand down. But that did not materialize, either. So we heard that if only the fractious Sunni and Shiite factions in the Iraqi government could have breathing space to reconcile their differences, and if only we could do more to blunt the force of the insurgency—that would be progress. To that end, in early 2007, the administration ordered a "surge" of tens of thousands more American forces to rein in the chaos in Iraq.

Today, we hear John McCain and legions of conservatives braying that we are, in fact, winning (some go so far as to say we have already won). Why? Because the "surge" has reduced the number of attacks on U.S. troops to the levels seen a few years ago (when the insurgency was raging wildly) and because there has been a momentary dip in the number of Iraqis slaughtering their fellow countrymen. Victory, apparently, requires only clearing out insurgents (for a while) from their perches in some neighborhoods, even though Teheran's influence in the country grows and Islamists carve out Taliban-like fiefdoms in Iraq.

The goals in Iraq "have visibly been getting smaller," observes John Agresto, a once keen but now disillusioned supporter of the campaign (p. 172). Iraq, he argues contra his fellow conservatives, has been a

---

This article originally appeared in *The Objective Standard*.

fiasco. "If we call it 'success,' it's only because we've lowered the benchmark to near zero" (p. 191).

Explaining the Iraq fiasco is Agresto's project in *Mugged by Reality: The Liberation of Iraq and the Failure of Good Intentions*. During 2003 and 2004, while the insurgency built momentum, he was a civilian adviser helping revive Iraq's higher education system. The book recounts his dealings with Iraqis and his observations on why a policy he had so passionately endorsed turned into a horrendous tragedy. What makes this book distinctive, and particularly illuminating, is its focus on the fundamental idea driving the war. While other Americans returning from Iraq have offered explanations for the problems in terms of superficialities—for example, the character flaws of specific officials or leaders—Agresto recognizes that the purpose of the Iraq campaign was to enact a specific ideal.

The point of the war, he writes, was not to enrich Big Oil, nor benefit Israel, nor "whatever the view of the month" happens to be. And while the Bush administration "may have had to highlight the issue of WMDs in its presentations before the U.N. and other international bodies . . . , finding and destroying such weapons was not something I or most of the civilians and soldiers I worked with in Iraq ever thought central to our going" (pp. 5–6). The goal was to fulfill the Bush administration's altruistic mission of lifting Iraqis out of tyranny and poverty and ignorance; it was, in Agresto's words, to "help secure the liberty of others" (p. 9).

By Agresto's own account, the military operations were prosecuted in compliance with the goal of serving Iraqis. He recounts the "surgical" bombing raids that spared much of the country's infrastructure. "The war was fought so precisely, so carefully," he observes, "that the only pictures of military destruction I was able to take while I was there were photos of former Ba'athist government buildings and military or communications facilities. The cities and towns were intact; homes and schools survived" (p. 173).

One of many appalling and little reported facts revealed in Agresto's narrative is that the devastation that "turned a country on the skids into rubble" was the work, not of Americans (as commonly believed), but of Iraqi looters. They marauded through "not just the universities, but all the schools, all hospitals, and virtually all public buildings, and not a few private homes." At Mustansiriya University, for instance, vandals ripped electrical wiring out of the walls and tore out plumbing fixtures; what they couldn't sell or use (e.g., books) they torched (p. 77).

The aftermath of the invasion itself left "no war-ravaged home-less rummaging through garbage cans, killing each other for crusts" (p. 174). On the contrary, he notes, "It would be hard to imagine a war fought, at the start, with greater care or with greater concern for non-combatants than Operation Iraqi Freedom" (p. 173).

Yet this care and concern, Agresto discovered, was not for the latent freedom-lovers he and so many others expected to meet.

In daily conversations with Iraqis from all walks of life, Agresto came to understand the Iraqi mindset. A number of anecdotal portraits and snatches of conversations reveal the typical Iraqi mind as profound-ly infused with pre-modern, tribalist religion. He encountered Sunni Iraqis (including a university professor) who openly voice a hostility akin to racism toward Shiite Iraqis, regarding them as sub-human, degen-erate heretics. Agresto tells of a Sunni man that he knew who went on the pilgrimage to Mecca and by chance found himself among a group of Shiite pilgrims. Hearing them sing a hymn expressing their unfavor-able view of the archangel Gabriel, the Sunni man was deeply revolted. "These people are not real Muslims," he told Agresto, "These people are heretics, all of them. They shouldn't be allowed to sing that." Then the man's voice grew darkly quiet, "They shouldn't be allowed" (p. 53).

Agresto's experiences in post-invasion Iraq disabused him of an ar-ticle of faith underlying the Bush crusade: the idea that there is a "uni-versal hunger for freedom" innately planted in all mankind. In reality, the prevailing ideological trend in Iraq—as in the Middle East general-ly—is totalitarian Islam (which he calls radicalized Islam). When Iraq's universities re-opened, Agresto reports, zealous students seized control, beating and murdering "un-Islamic" professors and other students. The power of Islamists on campuses—as throughout Iraq—grew so fierce that even female Christian students, in self-preservation, took to wearing Islamic headscarves. The Islamist enforcers worked in league with off-campus religious militias loyal to larger jihadist outfits, such as Moktadr al-Sadr's Mahdi Army.

It was not supposed to work this way: On the view of the Bush ad-ministration, once Iraqis were given the option, they would rush to em-brace liberty. Washington thus gave Iraqis a free hand to draft a new constitution. But the Iraqis enshrined Islamic law as the government's cardinal principle. The Supreme Federal Court of Iraq can overturn a law "not only if it violated the words of the constitution but also if it vi-olates 'the established provisions of Islam.'" This court, Agresto com-plains, is an imitation of the twelve-member theocratic "Guardians

Council" of the totalitarian Islamic regime in Teheran (p. 118).

Iraq, Agresto suggests, is steps away from theocratic rule.

What went wrong? Agresto blames the proponents of the campaign for failing to understand the Iraqi mindset. This step in his compelling argument brings to light important truths that proponents of the administration's policy evade. A telling example: Washington embraced Grand Ayatollah al-Sistani, spiritual leader of Shiites in Iraq, as a friendly, "moderate" political figure, but Agresto dismisses that view as deluded. The hugely influential cleric, it turns out, refused to meet with any Americans, but sat down with any anti-American antagonist. Demanding that all public legislation be based on Islamic law, Sistani condemned an interim Iraqi constitution because it protected the rights of the Kurds and secured property rights to Jews. The "very first time I heard, in all my months there, an anti-Semitic diatribe," recounts Agresto, "it was from the Grand Ayatollah. One word from Sistani might prevent the killing of journalists and Western civilians in Basra, stop the frightened exodus of Christians from all of Southern Iraq, and restrain the imposition of sectarian dogmatism now rolling over Iraq's schools and universities. There is no such word" (p. 101). Sistani, the book suggests, is a theocrat-in-waiting.

Agresto identifies a second factor toward explaining the situation in Iraq: the campaign was premised on a fundamental ideological confusion. He argues, passionately, that "democracy" and freedom are vastly different things. In criticizing the popular equation of democracy and freedom, Agresto observes that "elections are a means, not an end" and that there "is no alchemy in either the word 'elections' or 'democracy'" that transforms genocidal Islamists from bad to good (p. 99). Freedom in American, Agresto rightly points out, depends on the protection of rights. Freedom cannot be achieved, he argues, by unleashing (through elections) murderous Islamic mobs. In doing so, we have "handed Iraq over to exactly the worst elements" (p. 187).

The major value of the book lies in its exploration of how the war's theoreticians failed to understand both the Iraqi people and the American political ideas we were supposed to be enacting. Much of the narrative, however, is colored by Agresto's religious conservative views that man is moved by brutish impulses and that morality demands self-denial. These premises lead him to draw a broader conclusion that is unconvincing and inconsistent with the evidence he presents, and that seems grafted onto an otherwise trenchant analysis.

In keeping with his support of the campaign's selfless ideal, Agresto places blame—unjustly—on the character of the American occupiers: he reproves the U.S. servicemen implementing Washington's policies for caring more about themselves (!) than about the welfare of Iraqis. He concludes that Americans were not "ready to be the kind of liberating occupiers necessary to do the job right" (p. 182).

Taking this line of thinking further, he claims that the root of so much of the debacle can be traced to "a substratum of a baser human nature that Americans, and especially conservatives, seem forever eager to point out in theory, but forget about when confronted with in reality" (p. 182). The war's neoconservative architects "need to listen to more old-fashioned conservatives who know something about the fallenness of our natures," he admonishes (pp. 186-7). The ideal of serving Iraqis is noble, in other words, but it is beyond the ability of fallen, sinful creatures like us to be sufficiently selfless.

Yet the book fails to demonstrate this claim. The bulk of Agresto's narrative characterizes the mission as implementing, not betraying, Washington's ideal. Straining to support his claim, Agresto spends a chapter begrudging how little money the U.S. federal government (and other nations) gave away to pay for rebuilding universities. But given the Iraqi mindset that he describes, there is no reason to conclude that bestowing greater largesse on Iraqi universities would have averted the country's fall into barbarism. And for the same reason, the book does not and cannot explain how greater U.S. sacrifices, whether political, military or financial, could have brought about a peaceful new Iraqi regime.

In spite of the destructive results of America's selfless endeavor in Iraq, Agresto cannot bring himself to question his deepest moral beliefs, and instead he insists that the problem must be our fallen nature. In this respect he resembles the Marxists who explain away the brutality of Communist regimes by condemning humanity as depraved.

But the book's observant account of the early days of the Iraq campaign points toward a different conclusion entirely. It suggests that we should do what Agresto himself refuses to do: challenge the ideal animating Washington's war policy. That ideal, the events of the book indicate, is antithetical to America's self-defense (a point for which Yaron Brook and I have argued at length in "'Forward Strategy' for Failure," *The Objective Standard*, Spring 2007). *Mugged by Reality* presents gripping, vividly detailed—and at times moving—eye-witness testimony that should prompt Americans to call into question the altruistic ideal shaping our foreign policy.

PART 2

Learning the Wrong Lessons

Obama's Outreach Whitewashes Iran

Elan Journo   March 3, 2009

In his address to the joint session of Congress, President Obama said that "We cannot shun the negotiating table" in conducting our foreign policy. He's previously elaborated that "if countries like Iran are willing to unclench their fist, they will find an extended hand from us." And Iran's president Ahmedinijad tentatively welcomes "talks based on mutual respect and in a fair atmosphere."

The shared idea, evidently, is that our conflict with Iran stems largely from a past failure to use so-called diplomacy to settle disputes. Alluding to George W. Bush's supposedly tough policy, Obama has said he wants to restore "the same respect and partnership that America had with the Muslim world as recently as 20 or 30 years" ago.

Really? Thirty years ago this November, followers of Ayatollah Khomeini, who spearheaded Iran's Islamic revolution, stormed the U.S. embassy in Teheran and took the personnel hostage. President Carter gently admonished Iran, but ruled out military retaliation. Instead his advisors spent months dreaming up schemes to bribe Iran into releasing the hostages—while bending over backward to enable the regime to save face. In the end Khomeini's Islamist theocracy collected a handsome payoff for its aggression, and concluded, rightly, that if attacked, America would crumple to its knees.

Was Obama thinking of the 1980s? In April 1983 Iran's jihadist proxies in Lebanon rammed a truck bomb into the U.S. Embassy in Beirut; the Reagan administration responded by doing nothing. Months later, encouraged by Washington's inaction, Teheran issued a kill order—via its ambassador in Syria—to its allied groups in Beirut. Early one morning, an Islamist suicide bomber set off a massive explosion at the barracks where U.S. marines were sleeping and killed 241 of them.

Reagan spouted hot air about not backing down—and soon after ordered the U.S. troops to bug out. The jihadists wanted America out, they slaughtered our troops, and we caved in and gave them what they wanted.

Osama bin Laden, like jihadists in Iran and elsewhere, viewed our

---

This article originally appeared in *Capitalism Magazine*.

response to the Beirut bombings as further proof that their ideologically driven war was a viable cause. And so, inspired by Iranian aggression, the anti-American jihad kept ramping up.

Maybe Obama meant the fabled halcyon days of the 1990s, when President Clinton tried to mend fences with Iran?

In 1996 a team of jihadists—financed and trained by Teheran—blew up the Khobar Towers building in Saudi Arabia, killing nineteen American servicemen. Clinton's administration learned that Iran was behind the attacks. But Washington brushed aside any notion of retaliating against Iran, in order to facilitate a "reconciliation" with that murderous regime. In an eerie parallel with today, Iran expressed its openness to U.S. groveling—an opportunity Clinton seized.

So Clinton attended a speech by Iran's leader at the U.N.; the administration also permitted the sale of much-needed aircraft parts to Iran, among other sweeteners. Granted the cover of respectability, Iran was emboldened to continue fomenting Islamist aggression and avidly pursue its then-embryonic nuclear program.

Obama's appeasing diplomacy re-enacts the disastrous policy of the past. Our policymakers evaded Iran's character as an enemy, and by rewarding its aggression with bribes and conciliation, they encouraged a spiral of further attacks.

No. Bush was no exception to this trend. After 9/11 his administration invited Iran—the leading sponsor of Islamist terrorism—to join an anti-terrorism coalition(!). Talk of an axis of evil was quickly abandoned, and Washington backed the European scheme to bribe Iran to halt its nuclear program. By late last year, there was talk of opening a U.S. Special Interests Section (a step down from an embassy) in Iran. Meanwhile Bush's welfare mission in Iraq negated U.S. security and left Iran untouched to grow more powerful and resolute.

A genuinely new, rational policy toward Iran would turn away from the last thirty years and begin by facing up to Teheran's ongoing proxy war against us.

Obama's Solution for the Afghanistan-Pakistan Nightmare

Elan Journo April 6, 2009

In a speech announcing his "comprehensive, new strategy" for Afghanistan and Pakistan, Obama warned that "The situation is increasingly perilous. It has been more than seven years since the Taliban was removed from power [in Afghanistan, where they ruled], yet war rages on, and insurgents control parts of Afghanistan and Pakistan. Attacks against our troops, our NATO allies, and the Afghan government have risen steadily. Most painfully, 2008 was the deadliest year of the war for American forces." He may well have been understating the magnitude of the problem, particularly in Pakistan (considering a recent, brazen attack). And while both liberals and some conservatives have commended Obama's strategy (with minor qualifications), I regard it as fundamentally misconceived.

The strategy lays out what Team Obama claims are necessary steps to deal with the resurgent Islamists on both sides of the Afghan-Pakistan border. That action plan is based on certain assumptions about what went wrong. But that diagnosis, in my view, is false.

Let's start with one of the core claims in Obama's speech. What went wrong in the Afghanistan war? A major factor, according to Obama and many others, was the failure to send enough resources—primarily troops and financial aid. Moving forward, on this premise, "America must no longer deny resources to Afghanistan . . ."; and so Obama's sending 21,000 American soldiers into Afghanistan, and has promised boatloads of aid.

But this misses the underlying problem.

I've argued on other occasions that Washington's war failed because it was hamstrung by self-effacing battle plans. Our military was ordered to pursue Taliban fighters, for example, only if it simultaneously showed "compassion" to the Afghans. The U.S. military dropped bombs—but instead of ruthlessly pounding key targets, it was ordered gingerly to avoid hitting holy shrines and mosques (known to be Taliban hideouts) and to shower the country with food packages. The U.S. deployed ground forces—but instead of focusing exclusively on capturing or killing the enemy, they were also diverted to "reconstruction" projects for the sake of the Afghan population.

And this pattern continues today and is likely to intensify. The *New York Times* reported that "vast numbers of public, religious and historic sites make up a computer database of no-strike zones" while Air Force lawyers vet all air strikes.

The war put concern for the welfare of Afghans ahead of the necessary goal of defeating the enemy. Washington did not aim at smashing the Islamists, so instead they were scattered and left free to re-arm and fight another day. Sending 21,000-plus U.S. troops into Afghanistan will be of limited help—unless they are given new battle plans that entail the total defeat of the Islamists.

If only that were the focus of his strategy. But it's not.

Like the Bush administration, Team Obama believes that we must help the Afghans build a strong government. On the conventional analysis, it is the weakness and corruption of the post-Taliban regime that has contributed greatly to the chaos in that country. The idea is that if the Afghan regime were strong, it would serve as a bulwark against the Islamists. "Afghanistan has an elected government," Obama noted, "but it is undermined by corruption and has difficulty delivering basic services to its people."

Remedying this problem is at the center of Obama's strategy: he has promised to send approximately 4,000 U.S. troops to train the Afghan army and police and will exert pressure on the government to clean up its act. But will this really result in a regime that can oppose the Taliban? Sadly, the evidence suggests that what distinguishes the current government from the Islamists ideologically is only a difference in the degree of their fidelity to the principle of rule under Islam.

Consider some of the evidence. My colleague Tom Bowden recently noted the case of Afghans who were sentenced to twenty years in jail for modifying the Koran into Persian while not including the original Arabic text. That was blasphemous, you see. Or recall the fate of Abdul Rahman, an Afghan convert from Islam to Christianity: raging mobs and clerics demanded his execution. He was spared that fate by being spirited out of the country to Europe, but only because an international outcry embarrassed the government in Kabul. Keep in mind that these incidents are hardly isolated cases and that they took place under the supposedly pro-Western, pro-freedom regime—not the Taliban.

Moreover, the current regime has faced internal pressure to bend itself into greater conformity with the same Islamist political ideal—sharia—that the Taliban is fighting to impose by force throughout the country. There's an official council of Islamic clerics who advise

Afghanistan's president. Although their advice is nonbinding, they clearly wield tremendous moral clout. About a year ago, for instance, they demanded that President Karzai stop foreign aid groups from (allegedly) proselytizing for Christianity and that the government reintroduce public executions. Remember that the Taliban, when in power, kicked out foreign aid organizations and regularly put to death all who were deemed enemies of Allah (a practice that continues in the areas of the country where the Taliban regained control).

Among the council's other demands? The NYT reports: "The council also urged Mr. Karzai to stop local television stations from showing Indian soap operas and movies, which are enormously popular in Afghanistan but which it said included obscenities and scenes that were immoral."

Recall that the Taliban excelled at shuttering video-rental stores, tearing down satellite dishes, and "executing" TV sets—all in the name of promoting "virtue" and doing away with "immorality."

Take another example: Afghanistan's president recently signed the Shiite Family Law that "negates the need for sexual consent between married couples, tacitly approves child marriage and restricts a woman's right to leave the home." Sounds a lot like life under the Taliban regime, which among other things, of course, prohibited women from leaving home without a male relative. By signing the new law, President Karzai was apparently hoping to appease "conservative" lawmakers who drafted it.

So even if the improbable were to happen, even if Afghanistan's central government had a sufficient police force and military capable of enforcing the law of the land, that law is founded on Islam (according to the nation's constitution). And judging by current trends, there's reason to expect such a regime to veer toward ever more Taliban-esque policies. Ideologically, the regime has nothing to say in opposition to the doctrines of the Taliban, so how can it really oppose the Islamist resurgence? I don't see any grounds to believe that it could.

Obama's Destination? Non-Victory

Elan Journo August 4, 2009

July was the worst month for U.S. casualties in Afghanistan—not just in 2009, but since the war began nearly eight years ago. Keep this awful truth in mind as you read the following observation on that war from our nation's commander in chief:

"I'm always worried about using the word 'victory,' because, you know, it invokes this notion of Emperor Hirohito coming down and signing a surrender to MacArthur," Obama told ABC News.

Obama (echoing Bush) wants you to scale back your expectations: He's saying, "Don't expect us to break the enemy's will and compel it to surrender à la Japan in WWII." Whatever else America may be doing in Afghanistan, the goal is not to achieve anything like a genuine victory: i.e., the defeat of the Islamist enemy.

But why? Why might Obama and many other people hold this view? Two salient reasons come to mind:

(1) Since 9/11 the Bush administration has failed to properly define the enemy in the war. For a while it was "radical Islamists"; then "Islamofascists" for a week or so; "evil-doers" was in use for a while. The view that has stuck is that the enemy is al-Qaeda and the Taliban, a "shadowy," "non-state actor" (as Obama puts it). The conclusion that people draw: there's no enemy nation (à la Japan in WWII) for us to defeat, only scattered "terrorists." This conclusion is false and enormously destructive of our security.

(2) The Bush administration went to war, but it was a turn-the-other-cheek "compassionate" war, badly defined and lacking a clear objective (it should have been victory). The conclusion many have drawn: war was a disaster (look at Iraq! look at Afghanistan!), so forget war—it cannot be the answer. This conclusion is false, and it contributes to the debasing of our concept of what "victory" is, and how it can be achieved.

These two conclusions are part of the insidious legacy of the Bush administration's policy. And they're compounded by Obama's submissive, appeasing foreign policy. Consider what that means in practice: America sends its youth to die on battlefields—in a war that our leaders regard as unwinnable.

Must it be so? Could we triumph over the enemy? I believe victory is within our grasp—improbable as that may seem today.

To achieve a genuine victory requires a fundamental rethinking of how we got here. For a start, we'd have to define the enemy accurately, and then consider how to defeat it. That's a view I've advocated in some of my articles over the last few years. But there's a lot to say on this issue.

The fact that America's response to 9/11 has gone horribly wrong— and that we can, and must, defeat the enemy—was part of the motivation for the book project that I'm now wrapping up. The book, which I edited and contributed chapters to, is titled: *Winning the Unwinnable War: America's Self-Crippled Response to Islamic Totalitarianism*. Apropos of Obama's statement, quoted at the opening of this post, you may be interested to read the final chapter of the book. In it I describe a positive plan for how we could achieve a genuine victory—a victory on the model of World War II. The book is set to come out early this fall.

The Unending War in Afghanistan

Elan Journo   October 7, 2009

Today the war in Afghanistan reaches its eight-year mark. To put that into perspective, by now a child born on the day the war began would probably be starting his third year of elementary school. Or to put it in a wider context, only the American Revolution (which lasted about 8 years 4 months) and the Vietnam War (eight years six months) lasted longer. U.S. involvement in World War II was over in just under four years. The *New York Times* has a chart that illustrates these data in graphic terms. The Afghanistan debacle is on track to drag on longer than any of these. (I disagree with the compilers of this chart that the Iraq war is actually over; the recent bombings around that country suggest otherwise.)

Recall what many people agreed should be our (minimum) objective in Afghanistan eight years ago: the rooting out of the Taliban and its Islamist allies. Today a common view holds that we must resign ourselves to a world in which the Islamist menace remains a fixture of our lives—a threat we might mitigate, but never eliminate. Witness the suggestions by mainstream luminaries in foreign policy that we negotiate some sort of settlement with the Taliban, paying them to put down their arms, at least while we keep doling out cash.

That is not the punchline to a grim joke; it is what some consider to be our best option. The fact that this is taken seriously is a measure of how Americans have been demoralized by the failure of Washington to accomplish even the limited objective of eliminating the Taliban/al-Qaeda forces (to say nothing of dealing with the graver threat from Iran).

Iran's Fist, Clenched Tighter

Elan Journo   December 3, 2009

"[I]f countries like Iran are willing to unclench their fist, they will find an extended hand from us," Barack Obama suggested, nearly a year ago. Since then the Iranian regime has found itself inundated by the administration's cordial invitations (to a July Fourth barbecue; to talks over its nuclear program) and unctuous affirmations of our good will (see this video[1]). Even after the mass protests in Iran challenging the theocracy's legitimacy, Team Obama declined to lend its support to the protesters and thereby endorsed the regime that was gunning them down in the streets. By the logic of Obama's policy, all this should have induced Tehran put aside its "decades of mistrust" (of us), and halt its nuclear program and its patronage of Islamist terrorism.

So how's this working out?

Iran has just turned down the latest U.S.-backed deal meant to prevent it acquiring nuclear material suitable for a bomb. Instead, Tehran announced plans to build ten additional nuclear facilities on the scale of the one it already has up and running at Natanz. With that added capacity, it has been estimated that the Iranian regime could produce enough nuclear fuel for something like 160 bombs. Per year.

Then, over the weekend, the Iranian parliament passed a law "earmarking $20 million to support militant groups opposing the West." What's significant about this is not the amount of money, nor the fact that the government is officially budgeting for the sponsorship of Islamic terrorism (in the past Iran has spent tens of millions on Hezbollah alone). What's significant here is Iran's self-confidence.

Obama's policy of so-called engagement (read: appeasement) is working as predicted: it bolsters Tehran's militancy.

---

1. https://youtu.be/7tSpWLq8vVM

The Nobel Speech: Obama on "Just War"

Elan Journo   December 11, 2009

When accepting his Nobel Peace Prize—a ludicrous, debased award also bestowed on murderers like Yasser Arafat—President Obama spoke about his foreign policy. Pervading his Nobel speech there was a peculiar undertone of contrition. If translated into words, it would go something like this: "Ideally, we would behave like Gandhi, never resorting to the use of force in asserting our rights . . . but alas, as commander in chief of the United States, I'm duty-bound to protect the lives of Americans, and that now means having to fight. Sorry about that."

This apologetic drift flows naturally from the substance of Obama's foreign policy.

A key point in the speech is that America must uphold—but has lately fallen short of—the standards set by "just war" doctrine. Summarizing this widely held view of morality in war, he explains that a war is justified only "when it meets certain preconditions: if it is waged as a last resort or in self-defense; if the force used is proportional, and if, whenever possible, civilians are spared from violence."

> Where force is necessary, we have a moral and strategic interest in binding ourselves to certain rules of conduct. And even as we confront a vicious adversary that abides by no rules, I believe that the United States of America must remain a standard bearer in the conduct of war. That is what makes us different from those whom we fight. That is a source of our strength. That is why I prohibited torture. That is why I ordered the prison at Guantanamo Bay closed. And that is why I have reaffirmed America's commitment to abide by the Geneva Conventions. We lose ourselves when we compromise the very ideals that we fight to defend. And we honor those ideals by upholding them not just when it is easy, but when it is hard.

The implication is that Bush's policy was too assertive, was callous, and thus it undermined our interests and security. For these failings, Obama and many others believe, America owes the world an apology and a promise (delivered yet again in the Nobel speech) to change its ways.

But this is wrong. Massively wrong.

True: American foreign policy since 9/11 has been a disaster for our security; that's a driving point of my book, *Winning the Unwinnable War*. But the reason lies not in a failure to abide by "just war" doctrine; a significant part of the problem was Washington's devotion to that doctrine. My colleagues Alex Epstein and Yaron Brook demonstrate that point in chapter 4, where they bring to light the inherent incompatibility between "just war" and a victim nation's right of self-defense.

The "just war" doctrine, in modern form, dovetails with what I've characterized as Bush's "compassionate war." On this approach, Washington subordinated the military goal of defeating the enemy to the imperative of protecting civilians and nation-building Afghanistan and Iraq. The argument we present in the book is that this approach—now embraced, with greater dedication, by Obama—is destructive of U.S. interests. Of course warfare should be shaped by moral principles; the problem is that the dominant moral ideas of our culture, reflected in "just war" doctrine, subvert the self-defense of victims and work to the advantage of aggressors.

Obama's rededication to this way of thinking about war is like the logic of an alcoholic who works to solve his drinking problem by going on a binge.

Iran's Strident Defiance

Elan Journo December 17, 2009

President Obama has sought to buy off Iran with concessions and talks, so that Tehran will agree to end its nuclear program. This policy of so-called engagement (in reality, appeasement) has quite predictably shipwrecked (the administration is admitting as much). I have been arguing that Obama's policy of appeasement works to galvanize Tehran in its belligerence, including notably its nuclear program. That appears to be an intensifying trend.

Secretary of State Clinton starts making noises that the time has come to "pressure" Iran with the additional sanctions. Iran scoffs at a bill in Congress that would sanction its fuel supply. And it successfully test fires an enhanced long-range Sejil 2 missile.

Despite many layers of existing sanctions and restrictions on its access to foreign technology, "Iran has nevertheless learned how to make virtually every bolt and switch in a nuclear weapon, according to assessments by U.N. nuclear officials in internal documents" (*Washington Post*). Leaked documents purporting to be official Iranian reports describe "a four-year plan by Iran to develop and test a neutron initiator of a type that weapons experts say has no known civilian use." That initiator is one of the last technical obstacles on the path to developing a warhead.

Gloating in an interview, an Iranian official told the *Post* "that as Iranian engineers conquer the nuclear sciences, they will 'jump hundreds of meters up in a short time,' pulling even with their counterparts from the West."

Iran's nuclear program, however, is only one element in the regime's efforts to export and propagate its militant Islamist goal. Iran's proxies in that venture are jihadist groups. The leader of Hamas paid an official visit to Iran, which reaffirmed support for that group. Lebanese Hezbollah, another group that counts on Iran's patronage, has carried out attacks from Buenos Aires to Beirut, and is thought to have cells worldwide.

Speaking on another occasion, Ali Larijani, Iran's parliament speaker told reporters earlier this year: "We're proud to defend Hamas and Hezbollah," and "We are not trying to hide it."

What these developments illustrate is how the policy of appeasement rewards aggression, resulting over time in progressively more assertive, self-righteous enemies.

War on (Fill In the Misleading Blank)

Elan Journo December 24, 2009

One of the worst foreign policy developments of 2009 was also one of the most underreported—the Obama administration's decision to do away with the official use of the term "global war on terror" in favor of "Overseas Contingency Operation." The term "global war on terror" was awful, to be sure—it named our enemy vaguely and evasively. But instead of correcting that mistake by a clear identification of the enemy that threatens us with terrorism and nuclear attacks, President Obama's new designation denies the existence of any enemy. We went from worse to worser.

Correctly defining the enemy is indispensable in any war. My colleagues Alex Epstein and Yaron Brook write:

> To fulfill the promise to defeat the terrorist enemy that struck on 9/11, our leaders would first have to identify who exactly that enemy is and then be willing to do whatever is necessary to defeat him.
>
> Who is the enemy that attacked on 9/11? It is not "terrorism"—just as our enemy in World War II was not kamikaze strikes or U-boat attacks. Terrorism is a tactic employed by a certain group for a certain cause. That group and, above all, the cause they fight for are our enemy. [Chapter 4, *Winning the Unwinnable War*]

My colleagues and I define the enemy as the Islamic totalitarian movement—funded, inspired and backed by state-sponsors, principally Iran. We show how misidentifying the enemy by (one of) its tactics, terrorism, undercuts our ability to defend ourselves. "Terrorism"—and the host of other superficial definitions of the enemy ("evil doers," "haters," "hijackers of a great religion," etc.)—obscures the fact that the attackers were committed to an ideological movement, seeking the forcible imposition of Islamic law worldwide. The Bush administration's utter failure to properly name the enemy that threatens us is central to understanding why the U.S. response to 9/11 has been a fiasco.

Team Obama took this to a new low.

Apparently, "war on terrorism" retained some vestige of an association in the public mind with Islamist attacks—some faint hint of an ideologically driven state-supported enemy. The solution? "[M]ove away from the politics of fear toward a policy of being prepared for all risks that can occur," explained Janet Napolitano, Secretary of Homeland Defense. In a speech she gave, Napolitano deliberately avoided "the word 'terrorism,' [and instead] referred to '*man-caused*' disasters." [Emphasis added.]

This way of classifying mass-casualty acts of war, like 9/11, is an intellectual abomination. It works to dissolve any link between such violent attacks and the specific ideas motivating the killers. While clouding the intelligibility of the atrocities, this approach further underplays the moral culpability of those who carry them out. Moreover, and perhaps worse, it suggests that we ought to resign ourselves to attacks as if they were woven into the fabric of nature: we can no more eradicate the threat than we can eradicate earthquakes or hurricanes.

That defeatism was already becoming part of our culture in the final years of Bush's time in office; now under Obama it is being officially endorsed.

All of which underscores the crucial importance of correctly answering the simple, but momentous, question: Who is the enemy?

Disconnected Dots

Elan Journo January 12, 2010

L ast week, President Obama claimed that "our intelligence comm-
unity failed to connect those dots" signaling a plot to blow up
Northwest Airlines Flight 253, en route from Amsterdam to Detroit, on
Christmas Day. But ritual flogging of the intelligence community has
diverted attention from a larger failure—this one belonging squarely on
Obama's shoulders.

Zoom out from the plentiful red flags outlining what we already
know about the Christmas Day attack. Now observe the connection
between it and two (of many) other "dots": the suicide bombing by a
double agent at a U.S. base in Afghanistan; and the (latest) failed assassination attempt on the Danish cartoonist Kurt Westergaard, who
drew the Muhammad-with-a-bomb-in-his-turban cartoon.

On the face of it, these have little if anything in common. Unlike
the Nigerian bomber on Flight 253, the bomber in Afghanistan used
an explosive-packed vest; the assassin in Denmark wielded an ax. The
Nigerian was a recent college graduate, scion of a wealthy family; the
killer in Afghanistan was a doctor of Jordanian descent; the Danish
assassin, an immigrant from Somalia. Not their origin, not their specific targets, not their choice of weapon, not their age or income-level—
none of these are the same. Nor is there any evidence that they ever met.

But they do share an ideological bond that underlies—and
drives—their militant action. They belong to a movement that is waging a holy war to impose Islam as the supreme governing authority
over the totality of people's lives, by force and everywhere.

That's why the bomber sought to put to death a plane full of infidels on Christmas Day—as punishment for failing to embrace Allah
and as a gruesome spectacle vaunting the strength of the jihadist cause.

That's why the would-be assassin of Westergaard planned to hack
him apart: Westergaard's drawing had flouted Muslim dogma on
"blasphemy." So the assassin came to enforce sharia (Islamic law)—on
the totalitarian belief that sharia negates any freedom of speech under secular Danish law.

That's why the Jordanian double agent in Afghanistan felt it necessary to slaughter Americans, including seven CIA operatives: they
were working to capture leaders of al-Qaeda, one of many groups

advancing Islamic totalitarianism.

These are just three "dots" forming part of a larger picture. We face an ideological, militant movement that (I argue) is spearheaded by state-sponsors, chiefly the Islamist regime in Iran.

But it is a picture that the Obama administration refuses to bring into focus. Recall that after the Flight 253 attack, the president dismissed the bomber as an "isolated extremist" (a term perhaps even more evasive than "terrorist"). And observe the prevailing view that we're dealing with a multitude of separate problems—Iran, Afghanistan, random-seeming attacks on planes, etc.—that have to be dealt with piecemeal.

We have already seen how this approach plays out.

This myopic mentality, I argue in chapter 1 of my book *Winning the Unwinnable War*, is precisely the approach that dominated U.S. policy in the decades leading up to 9/11—decades punctuated with numerous Islamist attacks. The attacks were tagged vaguely as "terrorism" and each regarded as a separate crisis. The fact that there was a distinct ideological force behind these attacks went unrecognized and the enemy, undeterred.

Iraq's "Awakening" Re-Awakens Pro-Jihadist. Shocking.

Elan Journo   October 20, 2010

Much has certainly changed in Iraq since the nadir of the brutal civil war, but with increasing insurgent attacks, it's fascinating to see the actual consequences of the U.S. policies that were widely credited with delivering us a "success" (defined on a progressively debased standard of what counts as success; see part 1). Take the widely celebrated "awakening" of U.S.-backed Iraqis who turned against some jihadist groups. In my book, I assess that policy and critique it harshly. One problem: it is predicated on appeasement (the bribing of Iraqis to switch sides, so they turn against the jihadsts); another problem: it papers over the nature of conflicts among Iraqi factions and the deep-seated tribal/sectarian enmities. Here's a flavor.

> What happens when the torrent of cash [paid to members of the Awakening, "Sons of Iraq"] dries up? That future problem will sort itself out, we are told, because once stability is achieved, there will be a reconciliation among Iraq's warring ethnic and sectarian factions. The deadly gangland-style shootouts in the streets and ugly wrangling in parliament will cease, or so we have been promised. Washington believed that by arming and empowering the Sunni tribes, who constitute the bulk of the Sons of Iraq, it would pave the road for them to feel included in the nation's politics—which the majority Shiites now hold in a vise grip. Ultimately, the idea is to fold these gangs of former (and current) criminals, supposedly former jihadists, and ordinary Iraqis into the nation's Shiite-dominated police force. Some of that has happened, but the deep-seated, bitter resentment between Sunnis and Shiites in Iraq cannot be wished away. Many Sons of Iraq believe that their real enemy is the Shiite-run government in Baghdad, and with their American-provided arms, they await the day of reckoning.

What did that money buy? Allies who pledge their sacred honor to defeat Islamists? Consider this *New York Times* report from October 16 ("Sunnis in Iraq Allied with U.S. Quitting to Rejoin Rebels"):

BAQUBA, Iraq—Members of United States-allied Awakening Councils have quit or been dismissed from their positions in significant numbers in recent months, prey to an intensive recruitment campaign by the Sunni insurgency, according to government officials, current and former members of the Awakening and insurgents.

Although there are no firm figures, security and political officials say *hundreds of the well-disciplined fighters—many of whom have gained extensive knowledge about the American military—appear to have rejoined Al Qaeda in Mesopotamia. Beyond that, officials say that even many of the Awakening fighters still on the Iraqi government payroll, possibly thousands of them, covertly aid the insurgency.*

The defections have been driven in part by frustration with the Shiite-led government, which Awakening members say is intent on destroying them, as well as by pressure from Al Qaeda. *The exodus has accelerated since Iraq's inconclusive parliamentary elections in March,* which have left Sunnis uncertain of retaining what little political influence they have and which appear to have provided Al-Qaeda new opportunities to lure back fighters.[Emphasis added]

For my fuller critique of what was (and is) so wrong with America's "successful" policy in Iraq—and, broadly, what went wrong in Washington's post-9/11 policy—I encourage you to check out *Winning the Unwinnable War.*

Taliban's Morale

Elan Journo February 24, 2012

The Taliban and Islamist forces in Afghanistan have had their momentum reversed, their will to fight sapped—or so our policymakers would have us believe. But is that an accurate assessment? A new report from NATO, leaked to the *New York Times*, tells a far different story.

"The State of the Taliban" draws on 27,000 interrogations of 4,000 Taliban and other fighters, and it "portrays a Taliban insurgency that is far from vanquished or demoralized even as the United States and its allies enter what they hope will be the final phase of the war." Yes, very far from it: although more Islamist fighters are being killed or captured, many of those captured and interrogated "remain convinced that they are winning the war."

> The report, dated Jan. 6, provided little evidence to believe that this strategy or the increase in the number of troops during the Obama administration had helped spur the nascent peace talks. "Taliban commanders, along with rank and file members, increasingly believe their control of Afghanistan is inevitable," the report said. "Though the Taliban suffered severely in 2011, its strength, motivation, funding and tactical proficiency remains intact."
>
> It added of the insurgents: "While they are weary of war, they see little hope for a negotiated peace. Despite numerous tactical setbacks, surrender is far from their collective mind-set. For the moment, they believe that continuing the fight and expanding Taliban governance are their only viable courses of action."
>
> Recruits and donations for the Taliban increased over the past year, the report said, citing insurgents' accounts.

What's most alarming about the report, if it's accurate, is that the enemy, though materially weak, demonstrates far greater confidence than any enemy deserves to have after a decade of war with the United States, the world's most powerful military force. For a long time, and particularly in *Winning the Unwinnable War*, I've argued that to win a war, it's necessary to crush the enemy's will to fight, to leave the enemy feeling demoralized, convinced that its cause is lost. That's hardly what our campaign has accomplished. Why? A significant part of the answer lies in the way our own foreign policy has crippled our ability to defeat the enemy—and how we've boxed ourselves in so that we have few if any good options for how to proceed.

Is the report accurate? Obviously the captured fighters may be spouting propaganda that's been drilled into them. Even if that's what they're doing, that so many of them (some 4,000) have the confidence and morale to stay on message during interrogations is itself telling.

How the International Laws of War Subvert Self-Defense

Elan Journo November 2012

A Review of *Israel and the Struggle over the International Laws of War*, by Peter Berkowitz. Stanford, CA: Hoover Institution Press, 2012.

Israel is at the crux of a "new struggle over the international laws of war." So argues Peter Berkowitz, a legal scholar at the Hoover Institution, in his new and important book on the subject.

Exhibit A in Berkowitz's case is the United Nations' putative fact-finding mission on the 2008–9 Gaza war—an investigation which culminated in the notorious Goldstone Report. Exhibit B: the furor over the 2010 Gaza flotilla. According to Berkowitz, these and other incidents of maltreatment of Israel and efforts to criminalize the exercise of its right of self-defense "threaten[s] to effect legal transformations that will impair the ability of all liberal democracies to defend themselves."

By exposing what he regards as abuses of the international laws of war, Berkowitz intends to contribute to their defense. The book's evidence, though, renders that hope forlorn.

With lawyerly precision, Berkowitz dissects the Goldstone Report, highlighting the extent to which it is riddled with inaccuracies, half-truths, and Hamas propaganda uncritically reported at face value. For example, the report found that Israel illegitimately destroyed a family home in Gaza. But in reality, Hamas had used that home as a storage facility for weapons and ammunition, including Grad missiles, rendering it a legitimate military target. Moreover, in the eyes of the Goldstone team, Hamas is not a terrorist organization, but merely one of several "Palestinian armed groups." The report downplays the 8,000+ rockets and mortars launched from Gaza, as if they were causally unrelated to Israel's decision to retaliate. Berkowitz deftly argues that the report's application of relevant norms of war is legally unsound, and that its recommendation that the U.N. Security Council refer the matter to the International Criminal Court is baseless.

This article originally appeared in *The Journal of International Security Affairs*.

Procedurally, Berkowitz contends, the U.N. infringed on Israel's right to apply the norms of war when it prematurely authorized an investigation, before the fighting ended and before Israel could reasonably carry out its own preliminary assessments. Stoking suspicions that the investigation's verdict was a foregone conclusion, the U.N. General Assembly endorsed the Goldstone Report 114–18 (with 44 abstentions)—despite the report's embarrassingly numerous (yet thematically on-message) factual and legal defects. Curiously, nearly a year and a half later, Justice Richard Goldstone, who headed the investigation, retracted some of the most egregious claims; tellingly, however, the other U.N. team members unapologetically rejected the need to revise, let alone retract, the report.

What Berkowitz illustrates is a pattern wherein the international laws of war operate like a fulcrum for shifting blame from terrorists to the states fighting them.

This pattern was manifest in the outcry over the Gaza flotilla. That convoy, posturing as a humanitarian mission yet closely tied to an Islamist group, sought to pierce Israel's naval blockade of Gaza. After Israeli commandos boarded one recalcitrant vessel, the *Mavi Marmara*, a number of flotilla activists attacked them with axes, pipes and knives. Nine activists were killed in the process, and several dozen more were injured. The chorus of condemnation was instant and shrill and one-sided. The call for a U.N. investigation, Berkowitz observes, was intended not "to determine wrongdoing but rather to place an official stamp on Israel's guilt." The U.N. Human Rights Council—which has been notably mute over the years on incontestable violations of rights globally—bestirred itself to issue a resolution singling out Israel as the aggressor.

Critics warped the international laws of war to argue that Israel was forbidden to engage in the blockade, because it remained an occupying power in Gaza—even though Israel withdrew from Gaza completely in 2005, and Hamas violently took over the territory some two years later. Berkowitz convincingly demonstrates that Israel cannot legally be regarded an occupier, and, piece by piece dismantles the sophistry employed to deny the blockade's legitimacy.

Dismayed at how the international laws of war are deployed to undercut free nations, Berkowitz notes a paradox: no armies in the history of warfare have devoted greater attention than Israel and the United States to complying with laws of war, yet no armies today "come under greater worldwide attack for violating" those laws.

That moral inversion, Berkowitz suggests, could be rectified by clarifying and upholding the international laws of war. But on this point, the case is unconvincing. The laws of war are themselves deeply problematic. Take the idea, of which Berkowitz approves, that military retaliation must be "proportional" to the attack. Arguably, that precept stands at odds with a free nation's moral right to defend its citizens' lives. In the name of proportionality, should the U.S. retaliation for Pearl Harbor have been limited to bombing the same number of Japanese warships, and nothing more? Should Israel's retaliation against Hamas be confined to firing the same primitive, imprecise mortars at Gaza, and nothing more? Berkowitz calls for a "balance" between military necessity and the need to avoid civilian casualties. But surely the fundamental moral imperative must be the military objective, with the culpability for the unwelcome but sometimes inevitable collateral damage falling to the aggressor.

Compounding the problem is that the UN and related bodies enforce these so-called laws of war. It is not the Russias or Chinas or Irans of the world, but the United States, Israel, and a small number of other free nations that strive to comply with these laws, thereby lending them moral credibility. But the UN is dominated by authoritarian and terrorist-sponsoring regimes, making subversion of those laws all but assured.

Berkowitz assumes that the international laws of war are indispensable. The book's two case studies, however, should lead the reader to question that assumption. It is true that soldiers (indeed, all citizens) of a free nation need to have a sense of justice in their military cause. Yet moral guidance in war is the task not of some international organization but of a sovereign nation's foreign policy and moral principles; these should define the objective and appropriate means in a military conflict—just as they should inform decisions on alliances, treaties and international organizations. What Berkowitz advocates—championing the international laws of war but reserving prime responsibility of enforcement to nation states—leaves the moral high ground open for the usual suspects to seize it anew.

With this book, though, Berkowitz has masterfully exposed how the international laws of war have become a favorite bludgeon wielded against Israel. By bringing greater attention to the nature and provisions of those laws, the book serves as an urgent reminder of the need to scrutinize this doctrine and the international institutions that have become its champions.

How America and Israel Cripple Their Own Soldiers

Elan Journo   October 8, 2015

A horrific news report from Afghanistan brings to light a wider problem afflicting the American, and Israeli, way of war—but, no, it is not what you think.

Washington faces perpetual allegations of "war crimes" for its military conduct in Afghanistan, and Israel, in Gaza. We're asked to believe that U.S. and Israeli forces are overly aggressive, but that picture is perversely warped. The truth is that Israel and the U.S. wage self-crippled wars. To begin to understand that phenomenon, start with that sickening tale out of Afghanistan.

The practice of turning boys into sex slaves is rife in Afghanistan, reports the *New York Times*, "particularly among powerful men, for whom being surrounded by young teenagers can be a mark of social status." But if American soldiers and Marines in Afghanistan encounter that practice, they "have been instructed not to intervene—in some cases, not even when their Afghan allies have abused boys on military bases." Why?

Washington's turning a blind eye "is intended to maintain good relations with the Afghan police and militia units the United States has trained to fight the Taliban. *It also reflects a reluctance to impose cultural values in a country where pederasty is rife.*" (Emphasis added.)

Outraged at Washington's betrayal of individual rights, some American service members pushed back against the policy. But they "have been disciplined or seen their careers ruined because they fought it." (Read the whole story but be warned: it will turn your stomach.)

Such appeasement of an odious Afghan practice fits the pattern of Washington's self-effacing way of war. The proper objective in Afghanistan was to defeat whatever threat the Islamists posed, by crushing them militarily. And it entailed recognizing the unwelcome necessity of civilian casualties (for which the Islamists bear full responsibility). Instead, U.S. leaders waged a supposedly compassionate war that put the needs and welfare of Afghans first—ahead of the military objective. I document how this way of war played out in

This article originally appeared in *The Federalist*.

my book *Winning the Unwinnable War: America's Self-Crippled Response to Islamic Totalitarianism*. The ultra abridged version: It was a disaster. A few illustrations:

Washington's war planners defined lists of targets that were excluded from bombing missions. On these "no-strike" lists were cultural-religious sites, electrical plants—a host of legitimate strategic targets ruled untouchable, for fear of affronting or harming civilians. At the start of the war, American cargo planes dropped 500,000-odd Islam-compliant food packets to feed starving Afghans and, inevitably, jihadists. Bombing raids were often canceled, sacrificing the opportunity to kill Islamist fighters. The no-strike lists grew ever longer, giving the enemy more places to hide in and fight from. While handing the Islamists umpteen advantages, which they exploited, this self-crippled way of war tied the hands of American soldiers in combat zones.

That is how the Afghan war was actually conducted, because ultimately Washington believed we have no moral right to defeat the Islamists in the battlefield: the Afghan people had to come first. On that premise, who are we to assert the objective superiority of our moral values by standing in the way of Afghan men who turn boys into sex slaves?

Now imagine being an American soldier, witnessing an Afghan leader keeping a boy chained to a bed as a sex slave, and having to decide between complying with orders (ignore it) and doing the right thing (at minimum, speaking up). Defying orders could get you kicked out of the military and destroy your career. Contemplate the psychological toll of looking the other way and plugging your ears.

Soldiers face that same impossible choice—but with their own lives on the line—under the self-crippled rules of engagement on the battlefield. Over the last decade, I've met veterans of the Afghan and Iraq wars at my public talks. The insanely restrictive rules of engagement are maddening, they tell me: we were supposed to go after the enemy, risking our lives, but we were made to back off, retreat, and let them fight another day. Listening to them is heartbreaking. The tragic story behind *Lone Survivor*, recently made into a film, is emblematic. The injustice done to them, by the irrational policy of our leaders, has yet to be acknowledged. What must that do to their morale?

Yes, it is astounding that the world's most powerful military force actually pursued a self-crippled way of war.

But it is not alone: Israel, the Middle East's most powerful military force, has adopted essentially the same approach. Peter Berkowitz, a legal scholar, has noted the searing irony: the U.S. and Israel are widely accused of "war crimes" but in fact both "devote untold and unprecedented hours to studying and enforcing" the customary rules of war, which enjoin the avoidance of harming noncombatants.

Look at last year's Gaza war. Israel's paramount responsibility was to defend the lives of its own citizens. Morally, in defending itself, Israel's priority must be eliminating the threat from Hamas. Hamas declares its goal of destroying Israel in no uncertain terms. It is responsible for devastating suicide bombings and, over the years, thousands of rocket attacks from Gaza against towns and cities in Israel. Yet, against this backdrop—and mirroring the U.S. way of war—Israel subordinated the objective of self-defense in the name of safeguarding civilians in a war zone.

Recall, to take just a few examples, how the Israel Defense Force dutifully went far out of its way to warn of impending strikes. It dropped thousands of leaflets in Arabic warning Gazans to avoid certain areas that may be targeted. It phoned and texted people residing in apartment blocks where a rocket is about to hit, giving them time to evacuate. Often it fired "a knock on the roof" warning rocket, before leveling the building. It aborted missions if civilians were spotted nearby the target. Hamas notoriously stashed weapons, ammunition, and missiles in private homes. And it puts rocket launchers in densely populated areas.

Just as America hamstrung its own troops and drew up no-strike lists, handing a tactical gift to Islamists in Afghanistan, so Israel's conduct, shaped by the same premise, benefited Hamas.

Consider another parallel. Earlier this year, members of the Knesset read aloud testimony from Israeli soldiers who fought in the 2014 Gaza war. The aim was to rebut a UN report on supposed Israeli war crimes.

> "The [Israel Defense Force] followed all the rules to clear areas of civilians, but Hamas cynically forced some to stay," MK Dani Atar (Zionist Union) said, reading the testimony of a Golani soldier. "[Palestinians] were killed by explosives they didn't know were there that Hamas planted."
>
> "We lost our element of surprise, the best of our sons, to make sure we wouldn't kill civilians that the enemy used as human shields," he added.
>
> . . .
>
> MK Merav Ben-Ari (Kulanu) read a testimony by Dror Dagan, who was injured while arresting a terrorist, and listened from the visitors' gallery, sitting in his wheelchair.

"When we burst into the house and quickly scanned the rooms, the wife of the terrorist, a senior Hamas member, fainted. As a medic, I did not hesitate and started taking care of her," Dagan wrote. "Not two minutes passed and it turned out that it was a trap. It was all pretend, a trick to gain time so the suspect could get organized."

"I was injured, because I was taught the values of the IDF, to take care of anyone who is injured, even if it is the wife of a terrorist," Dagan added.

The cumulative aim of the statements was to illustrate—as if further evidence were needed—the tragic lengths to which Israel went to avoid harming civilians in the war zone. It's vital that the lies and distortions about Israeli military conduct be exposed and refuted.

But a fundamental problem common to Jerusalem and Washington is the underlying moral idea shaping their conduct of war. It is the idea that America (and Israel) ought to put their own interests last; that they must sacrifice the lives and security of their citizens to the enemies they are combatting. Both strive to conform to that prevailing norm. The more consistently they conform to it, the more they cripple their ability to engage in self-defense—the prime responsibility of a government to its citizens. The conventional norm shaping the conduct of war subverts free societies that abide by it, while enabling their enemies on the battlefield. Surely it is past time to rethink that way of war.

PART 3

The "Arab Spring," Islamist Winter

Egypt's Plight: "Moderates" to the Rescue?

Elan Journo February 3, 2011

In the streets of Cairo, tens of thousands are clamoring to get rid of strongman Hosni Mubarak. Ominously the Muslim Brotherhood—the origin of Hamas, al-Qaeda and other jihadist outfits—is maneuvering to assume leadership of the protests. The Brotherhood is our enemy; its success in Egypt means greater peril for us (to put it mildly). But some protesters evidently despise the Brotherhood's totalitarian political ideal. Where does that leave well-meaning Egyptians who want neither Mubarak nor the Brotherhood?

Beware of pinning your hopes on so-called political moderates. There are at least two related problems here.

(1) In the Arab-Muslim world, the slippery term "moderate" encompasses those who are merely anti-Islamist—not necessarily pro-Western. Many Egyptians readily swallow anti-Semitic, anti-Western conspiracy theories (e.g., the Protocols of the Elders of Zion). Moreover, supporting Palestinian "resistance" (read: terrorism) against Israel is a conventional, mainstream, uncontroversial view. Egypt is one of the places where ordinary people matter-of-factly will tell you that America got what it deserved in the 9/11 attacks. Keep all that in mind, when you ponder what it would mean for so-called moderates to be elected to power in Egypt.

(2) The other problem stems from the argument that so-called moderates can be a bulwark against the political power of Islamist groups like the Muslim Brotherhood. In that part of the world, the political spectrum is far narrower than you may think: whereas Islamists want religion to be the all-encompassing principle of government, a typical "moderate" still acknowledges that Islam has some, albeit limited, role in government. True secularists are scarce and marginal. So could "moderates" in government prevent the Islamists from taking over? Ultimately, no. I touch on this in my book, and here's part of the explanation.

> The only intelligible meaning of "moderate" advocates of religion are those who try to combine devotion to faith

with concessions to reason. They obey the dictates of Islam in some areas and not others, fencing off certain issues or areas of life from the purview of religion. Let us grant the premise that the West can find moderate Muslims and support them in a way that does not discredit them in Muslim eyes as saboteurs conspiring to undermine Islam. Could moderates really steer their culture away from the totalitarian movement?

The holy warriors hold that Islam must shape every last detail of man's life. The moderates accept the ideal of Islam but shy away from the vision of total state. Moderates might agree to allow sharia to govern schools, say, but not commerce; to dictate marriage laws, but not punishments for blasphemy, apostasy, or adultery. Yet in doing so, moderates ultimately advance the agenda of the totalitarians, since even delimited applications of Islam to government constitute an endorsement of it as the proper source of law.

The tension between moderates and the totalitarians is unsustainable. What happens when the totalitarians push for expanding the scope of sharia a bit more? If sharia can govern banking and trade, for example, why not other aspects of life? Why not also institute Islamic punishments, such as beheading apostates? Having accepted in principle the ideal of sharia, moderates have no grounds to reject further means to that end. They can offer no principled opposition to the slaughter of infidels who refuse to submit, or of apostates who claim the freedom to choose their own convictions. In the face of the incremental or rapid advance of the totalitarian goal, the moderates are in the long run impotent. If Islam is the ideal, why practice it in moderation?

One news report tells us that the ostensibly "moderate" Mohamed ElBaradei has talked about setting up a governing coalition with the Muslim Brotherhood.

The plight of Egypt—like that of much of the region—is intellectual. The protesters who genuinely do want a better future face no good options.

What could help Egyptians? To address that fully would take a separate discussion. At minimum, I'd name three things: the embrace of genuinely pro-freedom ideas, secular government and individualism.

Understanding the "Arab Spring":
A Conversation with Yaron Brook and Elan Journo

Journal of Diplomacy Spring 2012

How should the U.S. respond to the events that have gripped the Middle East over the past year? This question has been debated countless times by the media, academics, and politicians alike. Will the toppling of authoritarian regimes unleash a wave of democracy and individual freedoms across the region? Or will the power vacuums created allow darker forces to come to the fore? For a unique answer to these questions, the *Journal of Diplomacy and International Relations* looked to Yaron Brook and Elan Journo, both of the Ayn Rand Institute (ARI) in Irvine, California. Founded to promote the philosophy of twentieth-century novelist Ayn Rand—Objectivism—ARI advocates the principles of reason, rational self-interest, individual rights and laissez-faire capitalism. In the 2009 book *Winning the Unwinnable War,* both of these scholars argue for a revised U.S. foreign policy—one based on the principles that Ayn Rand stood for. To examine just what a foreign policy based on Objectivism would mean for the U.S., the *Journal's* Christopher Bartolotta and Jordan McGillis spoke with Yaron Brook and Elan Journo on the Arab Spring, American interests, Iran, China and much more.

Journal of Diplomacy: *The uprisings in the Middle East have received a lot of attention over the past year. Do you view these movements as a positive development for the United States and its interests in the region? How do you approach this situation?*

Elan Journo: When talking about U.S. interests, in the Middle East or anywhere else, we take a distinctive approach. We define the basic purpose of foreign policy as an extension of the government's proper function: to protect the individual rights of Americans to their life, liberty, and property. Our national interest, then, consists in safeguarding the lives and freedom of Americans in the face of foreign threats.

That stands in contrast to salient approaches in foreign policy—for

This interview originally appeared in the Seton Hall *Journal of Diplomacy and International Relations.*

instance, realism, liberal internationalism, and neoconservatism. Should we purchase the precarious, immoral friendship of some tyrant who tomorrow seeks to stab us in the back? No. Should we serve the world's have-nots with foreign aid, doling out grain, medical supplies, cash? No. Should we go on a crusade to bring ballot boxes to Iraq and elsewhere, à la Bush? No. Such policies, we argue, are at odds with—indeed, subvert—the goal of protecting the lives and freedom of Americans.

But, should we assert our interests—the safeguarding of the freedom of Americans—and should we use the full range of coercive options, including military force, in retaliatory self-defense when facing objective threats? Yes. Should we distinguish morally between our allies and enemies—acting consistently across time to encourage and support our friends, while shunning, ostracizing, and, when necessary, thwarting enemies? Yes. These key elements—the primacy of defending the rights of Americans, and the centrality of moral judgment in foreign-policy thinking—inform our approach.

To sum it up briefly, in our view, "U.S. national interests" reduces to the aggregate interest of American citizens to have their rights defended, to live free from foreign threats and attacks. We base our approach on the moral-political ideas of Ayn Rand, along with the founding principles of America.

Yaron Brook: When I look at the turmoil in the Middle East, the prospects are depressing. We have long been concerned that adherents of Islamic totalitarianism would rise to power. By the term "Islamic totalitarianism," I'm referring to many groups—the Muslim Brotherhood, al-Qaeda, Hamas, Hezbollah, and the Islamist regimes in Iran and Saudi Arabia. Despite their differences, what unites them as an "ism," as an ideological movement, is the ideal of enforcing the rule of Islamic law (sharia)—as an all-encompassing principle—and their ultimate goal (as far-fetched as it might seem to us in the West) of imposing sharia across the world—by force if necessary.

Today, the situation is far, far worse than even I would have projected when the protesters in Tunisia, Egypt, and elsewhere first took to the streets. Tunisia now has Islamists as leaders. Libya is heading in the same direction; the leadership of the anti-Gaddafi forces are Islamists, and they're likely to end up ruling Libya. If or when the Assad regime falls, it's the local chapter of the Muslim Brotherhood that's poised to take over. More dramatic and ominous, though, is the result of the Egyptian elections: the Muslim Brotherhood and the Salafis, combined, won the decisive majority of the votes in the first round.

Whereas for years the Brotherhood has sought an incrementalist strategy—creating a facade to appear less threatening, less fanatical—the Salafis are frank about their goals. They're far more open about what they want—and the Saudi-like, Taliban-esque way they'd like to impose Islamic dictates. They have been known to destroy stores that sell beer and cut off the ear of someone they accuse of committing sinful acts.

What we're seeing now in Egypt, Tunisia, and elsewhere is a swing from one form of tyranny—by a strongman or military clique—toward another form of tyranny, religious rule. For American interests in the region, every kind of dictatorship, whether an Islamist regime or a military-led police state, is inimical. Mubarak and Assad are horrifically evil tyrants; their rule is not in America's interest, nor obviously in the interests of Egyptians or Syrians. However, I strongly believe that the Islamists pose a much more serious threat, because they have an ideological agenda that is explicitly anti-American. Islamists view America, and the West, broadly, as an enemy, an obstacle to the realization of Allah's kingdom across the globe. On 9/11 we saw one Islamist faction, al-Qaeda, bring the holy war to American soil, hatching their plot in Taliban-ruled Afghanistan. Now project what we may face from holy warriors when more regimes in the region come under the sway of Islamist rule. The ascendancy of Islamists is the most important foreign policy threat facing us today.

JD: *The situation that you portray is quite grim, but some would argue that the revolutions are still in their early stages, and the possibility of fundamental political changes, changes for the better, cannot be foreclosed. Do you see room for that kind of change, long term?*

EJ: We should welcome political developments that bring greater freedom, meaning real respect for individual rights, for the people in that part of the world. We are better off when other nations truly move toward the protection of property rights, economic freedom, free speech—all of which are sorely lacking in the Middle East, with the notable exception of Israel. But for these political ideals to take root would require some fundamental changes in the political culture of the region.

What are the prospects for such fundamental changes? Doubtful. A major reason is the extent to which Islam permeates people's thinking and conceptual lexicon. Take Egypt. One explanation for why the Islamists did so well in the elections is that the Muslim Brotherhood was so well established, with a broad network of followers and organizers, and the ability to get out the vote. That's true, but a superficial explanation. It misses the real reason. The Salafis were far less organized politically, yet did remarkably well. Why?

What both groups have as an advantage over the quasi-secular groups is that the Islamists speak in the religious lexicon that all Muslims have been immersed in, even if they themselves are far from devout. Try advocating a separation between state and religion—something unknown through most of Muslim history; when it became known through contact with the West, it was shunned. If you advocate a separation of state and religion, you'll face resistance. If you advocate a secular state, the Islamists easily undercut it by portraying it as Western, and discrediting "secular" by tying it to pseudo-secular dictators, like Mubarak and Assad, who have ruled for decades. The Islamists can easily vilify "secular" as immoral, even repressive. So secular-oriented activists have to talk in vague terms such as "civilian state" lest they appear to advocate an impious society. The sheer fact that you can discredit something by tagging it as Western is revealing.

That illustrates two things. First, it's the religious groups that set the terms of debate, because they couch their arguments in moral terms, terms that resonate with a broad swath of the populace. Second, there's little understanding of what secular society looks like—a fact evidenced in history by the dearth of terminology in Muslim lands to describe and conceptualize it, and in the present by the implicit equation of secular, or non-religious, with immorality. The few marginal, secular-leaning advocates are thus on the defensive, for fear that they be tarred as enemies of virtue and Allah's law. Islam's cultural influence provides a huge advantage to Islamists.

Another factor here is that for the last few decades, the region has seen a trend of increasing religiosity—a trend that Islamists both help to drive and benefit from politically. Many people see themselves first and foremost as Muslims, rather than as individuals, or even citizens of their country. They identify themselves more closely and consistently by their adherence to Islam. More Egyptians go to prayers. More mosques are sprouting up. According to one report I've seen, in 1986 there was one mosque for every 6,000 or so Egyptians. Nineteen years later—and after a doubling of the population—there was one mosque for every 700 or so people. More women are donning the hijab—without being coerced into it by state-run "morality police." Amid an increase in religiosity, it is the ideologues of Islamic totalitarianism, espousing the need for restoring piety, who stand to gain not merely a respectful hearing, but also followers.

YB: There's another important point in thinking about what it would take for fundamental political changes to emerge in the Middle East. One of the essential pre-conditions for a civil, rights-respecting society to emerge is a respect for individuals as sovereign. By that I mean each person is seen as entitled to his or her own life and freedom, to live by the judgment of their own mind—by right, not by the permission of the state, the imam, or the tribe. This is the principle on which America was founded and that today we in America, and the West, broadly, accept. That represents significant moral-political advance, a measure of progress in human civilization. To give an example: if my twenty-something son comes home to tell me he's going to marry his girlfriend, whether I like it or not, it's his choice—both morally and politically.

Go to a conventional family in Cairo: you'll find that who a son will marry is often a decision the parents, and other members of the clan, will make. What he wants is extraneous. Who a daughter may marry is conventionally the exclusive prerogative of the family, because the family, sometimes the tribe, as a collective, comes first. What the girl wants or doesn't want is irrelevant. Is she sovereign? Clearly not.

What I'm describing here is not a quirk limited to marriage decisions; it's an illustration of a broader cultural reality, namely, the subordination of the individual to the larger family or tribal group. So long as this kind of collectivized outlook is endemic in a culture—and it is in Egypt and across the region—it's hard to imagine the successful advocacy, let alone the enforcement, of new laws to protect the freedom of individuals to act on their own judgment.

The upheavals in the Middle East have toppled dictators, but there's no evidence of a change in the fundamental ideas or outlook of the populations. On the contrary, we've seen an entrenchment of the worst prevailing ideals.

JD: *The Obama administration does not seem to have a coherent policy toward these various uprisings, and often has a different policy toward each state—for example, it took a far more active role in Libya than in Egypt. Do you believe that this was a rational policy, to view each uprising independently, or would a coherent strategy have been more beneficial?*

EJ: Behind the incoherence is something else, worse and little understood. What we've witnessed is the impact of ideas in morality on the thinking and practice of U.S. foreign policy. Yaron and I have long argued that certain common moral ideas have subverted U.S. policy—that's the theme of my book examining the Bush administration's post-9/11 policy. The Obama administration is likewise operating under the guidance of certain ideas about morality that lead to bizarre, and destructive, policy decisions. You can see that if you compare the U.S. response to the uprising in Libya with the response to the post-election protests in Iran, a couple of years ago.

Libya under Gaddafi was a trivial threat to our security. Who the protesters were and what political goals they sought—we didn't inquire, but we nonetheless backed them with airstrikes and other forms of military support. We stated no clear purpose for our involvement in enforcing a NATO-led no-fly zone; morally, we took our cue from that infamous club of tyrants, the Arab League; practically, we subordinated ourselves to the Europeans. From top to bottom, no significant U.S. interest was at stake. There was no evidence that our involvement in the mission would advance our interest—and in fact, all the evidence suggests that it has empowered a new, militant Islamist regime. The Libya mission was diametrically opposed to the goal of protecting the rights of Americans.

Now, recall the massive protests in Iran two years ago. The Iranian regime is designated by our State Department as the most active state sponsor of terrorism. Through proxies like Hezbollah, the Islamist regime in Tehran has committed many acts of aggression against the United States and other Western interests. Its Revolutionary Guard Corps helped create and train Hezbollah, which hijacked a TWA airliner and which kidnapped and tortured to death Americans. Iran was behind the 1983 bombings of the U.S. Embassy in Lebanon and later the barracks of U.S. Marines, killing 241. Iran also orchestrated the 1996 car bombing of Khobar Towers in Saudi Arabia, where nineteen U.S. servicemen died. That's just a glancing indication of what should be thought of as a multi-decade proxy war against us.

So, in Libya, we move against a minor, tin-pot dictatorship where we have no real stake, while leaving the fire-breathing Tehran regime in place, implicitly endorsing its rule by neglecting to help the protesters. In Libya, we launch bombing raids, for the sake of civilians and rebels whose goals are at odds with ours, against a regime that's of minor significance to our security. But against a major threat to us, from Iran, we stand mute and idle.

When our interests are in fact at stake—as they were and are in

Iran—we hold back and take an accommodating line toward the belligerent regime. When someone else's needs appear to be on the line (the rebels and civilians in Libya), we dutifully scramble jet fighters and put American lives in harm's way, for the sake of serving others. Why? That double standard has its roots in the prevalent moral view that permeates our foreign policy—a view requiring that we put the needs of others ahead of our own goals and interests.

Acting in accordance with that view has been enormously destructive to American security and freedom, across decades. To expand on this a bit, part of what we've argued about post-9/11 foreign policy is that much of it stemmed from the idea of putting the supposed need of impoverished, oppressed Iraqis to have the vote, ahead of our interest in eliminating actual threats to our security (from known enemy regimes, like Iran). We argued that the Bush campaign to bring elections to the Middle East was wrong, morally. There's much more to say about that, but the macro point here is this: underlying the chaos that passes for U.S. foreign policy are commonly held ideas in morality that are at odds with the goal of protecting the lives and freedom of Americans.

JD: *You have both written that America's real enemy in the world today is Iran. What is the reasoning behind this statement, and what are the implications for how the United States has been conducting its War on Terror?*

EJ: I'm not claiming Iran is our only enemy, but it is a significant one, because Iran is the standard bearer for the Islamic totalitarian movement. The regime in Tehran embodies the totalitarian ideal and actively seeks to expand its dominion, by force. Since the revolution that gave birth to the Islamist rule in Iran, the regime has inspired Islamist groups across the world by exemplifying their political goal.

Inseparable from that is Iran's efforts to export its Islamist revolution—by inspiring, funding, and supporting proxies and affiliates like Hezbollah—and proving that it can attack America (through proxies and directly) and get away with it. By doing that, Iran purports to show that a truly pious regime can best an infidel superpower, America. Earlier we touched on the long record of Iranian-backed attacks on Americans, beginning with the 1979 seizure of the U.S. Embassy in Tehran. I lay this out in detail in my book *Winning the Unwinnable War.*

When assessing the Islamist threat, part of what makes Iran the salient state-sponsor is the fact that it eagerly seeks the mantle of leading the so-called jihad on the West. Given the regime's past aggression and current belligerence, Iran definitely poses a threat to the individual rights of Americans. Though not the exclusive patron of the Islamist movement—Saudi Arabia and Pakistan are a serious problem too—Iran's funding and ideological inspiration for the movement is crucial. Without it, the movement would be largely impotent.

YB: Since 9/11 there's been massive confusion about the nature of the enemy that struck us. The Bush administration failed to properly define the enemy, and compounded the confusion by championing the term "war on terror"—singling out a tactic as our enemy. The enemy in fact is an ideological movement—what we define as Islamic totalitarianism.

You asked about some implications of our view for how America has responded to 9/11. *Winning the Unwinnable War* deals with that at great length, but to offer a snapshot, consider one key point. The failure to properly define the enemy, and thus to grasp Iran's centrality within the Islamist movement, meant that U.S. policy instead focused on other, I believe lesser, threats—notably Iraq—and left Iran, for the last ten-odd years, to continue its proxy war against us. Our policy served only to encourage Iranian belligerence—witness its backing of insurgents in Iraq, its reach into Afghanistan, and of course its nuclear quest.

JD: In light of the November 2011 IAEA [International Atomic Energy Agency] report, the general international consensus is that Iran is building a nuclear weapon. Given that, what should the policy of the United States be?

EJ: We must recognize that Iran's quest for nuclear capability is neither new nor an anomaly from its past goals and actions. It is part of an ideologically driven campaign to export its Islamic revolution and gain the means to inflict harm on what Tehran regards as its enemies. Iran has for decades backed terrorist proxies to carry out attacks using conventional means—guns and bombs. So, even if Iran never acquires nuclear capability, the fundamental problem is the belligerent regime and its ideological agenda.

YB: How should we deal with this situation? The chief complicating factor is that for thirty-odd years we have turned a blind eye or reached out an appeasing hand to Iran after each of its attacks. That has in many ways allowed the regime to grow stronger and encouraged its militancy. The problem has festered for so long that we've passed the point where non-military solutions could be effective. We failed to act early, and we've been paying for it.

The 2009–10 protests in Iran offered the possibility of a non-military way of replacing the regime with one that's less- or non-threatening. But the administration squandered that opportunity. I see no real solution without using military force.

But to be clear: what I'm referring to is nothing like what the United States did in Afghanistan or Iraq. Those campaigns were far from the kind of war necessary to eliminate a threat; as Elan and I write in the book, those campaigns are best characterized as essentially "welfare" missions, where the priority in reality was not to eliminate whatever threat the regime posed, but rather to fix up hospitals, clear sewers, and deliver ballot boxes.

The kind of military action I believe is necessary in the case of Iran is far, far different. The exclusive goal would be to end the threat—not an open-ended nation-building crusade à la Bush. One consequence of Iraq and Afghanistan is that people can scarcely imagine that military action can actually succeed in delivering peace—as it did, for example, in World War II. Lately in the foreign-policy establishment some have argued that a nuclear-capable Iran is something we can live with, something we could cope with through "containment." It worked with the USSR, they tell us, because of the fear of "mutually assured destruction," so we can count on the same approach to checkmate the threat of a nuclear Iran. I disagree.

The analogy with the communists completely breaks down, because the Soviets at least wanted to live on earth; the fear of mutual destruction could deter them. But an essential characteristic of the Islamist regime in Tehran is that its ideology celebrates martyrdom and glorifies the afterlife. Can we trust containment to succeed in the face of that kind of mentality? No. There are other reasons why containment is untenable—among them the risk that neighboring regimes, themselves politically unstable and unfriendly, will immediately seek nuclear capability, too. The bottom line is that Tehran's ideology is the problem—it's the driving force behind Iran's decades of aggression. Ultimately, only changing that regime can eliminate it as a threat. The hope is that there would be enough Iranians who oppose it from within, capable of establishing a successor regime that is at minimum a lesser or non-threat to the United States.

JD: *You mentioned Saudi Arabia as another problem regime. Many have hailed the "special relationship" between the U.S. and Saudi Arabia, claiming that the Saudis are a great U.S. ally in a tumultuous region. But is this really the case? Is Saudi Arabia a great ally of the U.S. or is it actually a covert enemy?*

EJ: The Kingdom of Saudi Arabia is regarded as a loyal U.S. ally, but that standing is undeserved. Within its borders, the regime governs by reference to sharia. Its youth are inculcated, in schools, through state-controlled media and mosques, with hatred for Western values such as political freedom. Regime-endorsed religious leaders deliver anti-American diatribes at Friday sermons. Preachers in mosques, online, and on television incite Saudis to engage in jihad. It works: fifteen of the nineteen hijackers on 9/11 were Saudis. Many insurgents in Iraq came from Saudi Arabia. Moreover, many billions of dollars from Saudi Arabia are channeled through the world to proselytize for the regime's Wahhabist strain of totalitarian Islam.

This is a regime that espouses political ideas opposed to ours and in league with those of the Islamic totalitarian movement. The regime tramples on the rights of its own people. And it funds and advances the spread of Islamist ideas globally.

The U.S.-Saudi relationship is emblematic of the kind of problems in U.S. foreign policy that we've already touched on, particularly the need to assess other regimes objectively and deal with them accordingly.

JD: *In today's world, oil is a most precious resource, but many would argue that our dependence on foreign oil is actually enriching our enemies in the Middle East. Do you believe that this is the case? And how should the U.S. restructure its energy policy to ensure its national security while at the same time not hurting the purchasing power of its citizens?*

YB: To be clear: I'm in favor of our using oil and gaining access to it from the Middle East. But in doing so, we cannot compromise on our own political ideas—chiefly, the principle of individual rights. We cannot pretend that the Saudis are better than they are. We cannot appease them and flatter the regime with undeserved praise.

Yes, obviously petrodollars go toward funding the Islamist movement. But that's not an argument to deprive ourselves of oil, the lifeblood of our modern civilization. Rather, it's an argument to deal with the Islamist threat head on. Even if it were feasible to reduce our use of Middle East oil—which for technical reasons is nontrivial—that's woefully insufficient to stop Islamic totalitarianism. To stop it requires not only uprooting the movement's logistical-operational network, but, more important, demonstrating to its adherents that their cause is lost. That requires far more than a squeeze on their cash flow. It requires crushing the enemy's will to fight. That can be done by instilling in them a fear of acting on their political goals—a fear that if they act, they will face overwhelming retaliation. Part of the problem lies with state-owned natural resources. Properly, they should be privately held—both here in the United States and everywhere else in the world. State ownership of such resources is all the more problematic when the regime is autocratic or dictatorial. In the book, we talk about how we could accomplish our goal of securing access to oil. I'd argue that the ability to purchase oil is important enough to our prosperity that we should not rule out using military coercion to ensure the flow of oil. One of many ways to do that is to lay down a firm ultimatum to Saudi Arabia, that it must halt all backing for Islamists and assure the export for trade of oil, or else face our military might and, say, have all of its oil facilities privatized and overseen by us.

JD: *An under-reported issue that seems to have escaped media attention is the fact that U.S. troops are now fighting in Uganda. Coupled with the recent intervention in Libya, what does this say about the way in which the government is now using the military? Are these new conflicts being fought in the interest of the American people?*

EJ: The Uganda mission illustrates an earlier point about U.S. foreign policy: how one conceives of U.S. interests determines the kind of policy one advocates. In our view, the guiding principle is the protection of Americans' individual rights. Are those imperiled by the situation in Uganda? Is the Lord's Resistance Army (LRA), the group that our mission aims to help bring down, an objective threat to our lives or property? No, and I've yet to see anything like a decent argument for that.

Our view is that such a mission fails to meet the standard of advancing U.S. interests, i.e., of safeguarding the lives of Americans. What the LRA is doing is abhorrent, without doubt. But I'd argue that it is not our responsibility to intercede in this conflict. Nor is it moral to put U.S. servicemen in harm's way, for the sake of so-called humanitarian missions.

But like similar missions in the past, what motivates it is a common viewpoint that America, because it is strong and wealthy, has a moral duty to serve the weak and poor, to act as a combination global policeman and social worker. If one were to implement this viewpoint consistently, there's no end to the foreign conflicts that we would be obliged to provide help for. How could turning our military into a global social-services organization ensure our security? It cannot. In fact it squanders our means of protecting ourselves. Ultimately, that's a self-sacrificial policy.

JD: Some scholars have speculated that the Arab Spring will eventually spread to China, where we will see a popular movement against the Communist Party and in favor of democracy. Is it in the interest of the United States to support a democratic movement in China? Would it be possible to do this without antagonizing the Chinese government?

YB: I would not say that the so-called Arab Spring is spreading to China. First, the term "Arab Spring" packages together dissimilar events, and it's far from obvious that the implied positive evaluation is warranted: were they uniformly or unambiguously pro-freedom? Hardly. Second, pro-freedom activists in China have mounted protests in various forms at least since 1989. Given political developments in China over the last decade, I would not be surprised if there were an increase in such activism in China.

It is proper for our policy to lend moral support to people who seek greater freedom—wherever they are. That means speaking up in defense of those who genuinely fight for their individual rights. America's moral authority is considerable, but we hardly ever pull our weight by making confident, morally unambiguous declarations of support for true freedom activists.

Lending moral support to pro-freedom activists is an underappreciated means of asserting U.S. interests around the world. Talk to people who lived in the former communist bloc, and many will tell you how powerful an inspiration it was to know that the free world was on their side and recognized their plight. The pro-forma utterances from the White House and State Department, which today pass for statements of moral support, are pathetically meek and therefore ineffectual.

Let me add parenthetically that we should only ever provide military support to pro-freedom causes or nations when there is objective evidence that the rights of Americans are directly threatened, such that it becomes a matter of our self-defense.

What would happen if we actually spoke up for genuine pro-freedom activists in China? It would likely antagonize Beijing. But so what? A principled moral stand in favor of freedom will make us safer, long term—whereas the perception of U.S. weakness and our own irrational policies are a considerable threat to our security.

JD: Many people see communist China as the next enemy of the U.S. But China is by far the U.S.'s largest trading partner, and has an enormous impoverished population that could one day grow and enhance that relationship. Should the United States view a rising China as a threat or as an opportunity?

YB: History has taught us that authoritarian governments are potential enemies, because a regime that violates the rights of its own citizens may feel little or no compunction about trampling on the rights of people beyond its borders. But I don't view China today as an enemy of the United States, though it was once, and could become one again. One legitimate fear is that the Chinese economy stalls, and the regime decides that sparking a conflict with the United States would distract the impoverished population from their economic misery. It's important to recognize that what could make China a military threat is the authoritarian character of its government—not the growth of its economy.

Trade with China is not a threat to us, but rather a voluntary exchange of goods and services to mutual advantage—it's a win-win relationship. We benefit enormously from China's economic growth and success. The more they create and trade with us, the better off we are. But China's long-term economic success is unsustainable unless there is greater political freedom for its people—unless the authoritarian system is abolished. On this point both we and the Chinese people have the same long-term interest: to see China's eventual transition to a free and therefore increasingly prosperous country.

JD: The debt crisis in Europe obviously has large implications for the U.S. and the international financial system. What do you see as the root cause of the financial crisis and the current debt crises threatening the West?

YB: There's more to say about this than I can address fully in our conversation. My colleague Don Watkins and I have a forthcoming book that deals with these and related questions at length. Let me touch briefly on a few key aspects.

Ultimately, behind these economic crises is a moral-political issue: What is the proper role of government? Contrary to conventional wisdom, the system of government that prevails in the West is not, strictly speaking, capitalism—meaning a system in which there's a separation of state and economics. Rather, we have an unstable mixture of some freedom with massive—and growing—state intervention and entitlement programs. The prevailing view holds that government must intervene, regulate, centrally control, and provide handouts and bailouts.

What Don and I argue in our book, in our Forbes.com column, and elsewhere is that the regulatory policies of the federal government are the root cause of the financial crisis—from beginning to end. Obviously, it's an involved story, but a key dynamic in the crisis was the interplay of two long-running policies that spanned both Republican and Democratic administrations: we had a destructive combination of artificially low interest rates and a long-standing campaign to encourage as many people as possible to buy homes. There were other factors, and they too stemmed from the distortions in the financial markets that arise only because of regulatory policies and expected state interventions (e.g., "too big to fail").

Europe is facing a crisis born of its welfare-entitlement system. European governments promised welfare benefits, pensions, health care, wages for public employees, etc., that they cannot afford to pay from tax revenues. Until recently the governments borrowed money to cover the shortfall—but that was unsustainable. Markets eventually realized that at current rates of spending, many European governments would never be able to pay their debts.

America's own entitlement programs—Social Security, Medicare, Medicaid—are a massive unfunded liability that constitutes the lion's share of government spending. Unless we dramatically cut spending on entitlements, we too risk suffering a fate like that of Greece. The problem today is what you could describe as an unlimited government that is enmeshed in all aspects of the economy. If we leave that problem unaddressed, the crisis will continue. It will spread across the developed world. And it will become more severe.

What's needed to re-orient the U.S. economy onto the right track? Massive cuts in government spending, the phasing out of entitlements, real deregulation of business—in other words, a fundamental change in how we view government's role. We need to return to a government that does only one thing, but does it well: the protection of our individual rights to life, liberty, property and the pursuit of happiness.

Islamist Winter

Elan Journo   November 2013

A Review of *Spring Fever: The Illusion of Islamic Democracy*, by Andrew McCarthy. New York: Encounter, 2013.

Early on, the conventional view on the so-called Arab Spring was euphoric. In a nutshell, it was that the upheavals herald the triumph of freedom. Two-plus years on, however, Islamist groups have gained considerable political power—an ascendancy ominous not only for those subjugated under sharia, but also for American and Israeli security. Searching for silver linings on a darkening horizon, some point to Turkey: here is a regime widely feted as proof that Islamist rule is compatible with political freedom, after all.

Andrew McCarthy roundly refutes that view in *Spring Fever*. Recep Tayyep Erdogan's regime, he contends, serves as a case study of what to expect of ascendant Islamists in the Middle East: more oppression, and more hostility toward the West. "The trend-lines are unmistakable," he writes, "the trajectory of change more certain than its pace."

Turkey's Islamization hinges on the way Erdogan, like his Islamist brothers-in-arms, exploits the West's uncritical embrace of "democracy." McCarthy reports how, four years before his party assumed power, Erdogan explained that "Democracy is just the train we board to reach our destination." The ploy: feign an interest in freedom, then once in power shift toward Islamist rule.

Erdogan's incrementalist campaign aims to remake Turkey's institutions. He prioritized Islamic over secular education, encouraging greater enrollment in religious academies, and seeded the universities and government posts with Islamists. With religious mores—notably public displays of piety and the subservience of women—becoming the new normal, women withdrew from the workforce in droves. The rate at which women are murdered (including "honor killings") has rocketed upward by 1,400 percent. For women aged 15 to 44, "gender-based violence" is now the leading cause of death (far outstripping cancer, traffic accidents, war and malaria).

This article originally appeared in *The Journal of International Security Affairs*.

Erdogan also replaced some 40 percent of Turkey's 9,000 incumbent judges with loyalists who embrace the Islamist agenda of his Justice and Development Party (known by its Turkish acronym, AKP). And, openly subverting rule of law, he selectively refuses to enforce uncongenial judicial rulings. Critics of the regime have found that freedom of speech is largely a mirage. Challenge the regime's authoritarian control, and you risk being intimidated, detained, framed, and jailed. Last year, Ankara earned the horrifying distinction of having imprisoned more journalists than any other country (more than Iran, more than China). (When an Istanbul park became the epicenter for nationwide protests this summer, the major news outlets were conspicuously silent. And in the brutal crackdown on the crowds, the regime's authoritarian essence was on full display.)

It is in Turkey's foreign policy that McCarthy discerns a stark "transition from the Western to the Islamic sphere." Ankara once cultivated strong economic bonds and military cooperation with Israel. That relationship has frayed. Under the ironically labeled "Zero Problems with Neighbors" policy, Erdogan's regime has befriended Hezbollah, embraced Iran's jihadist leadership, and openly supported Tehran's nuclear program (even resisting attempts to impose UN sanctions against it). A particular favorite is the Palestinian jihadist group Hamas. "I don't see Hamas as a terrorist organization," Erdogan insists. "Hamas is a political party." In 2010, the Gaza Freedom Flotilla, aiming to breach Israel's blockade of Gaza, sailed with Ankara's blessing. Erdogan has hosted Hamas leaders as visiting dignitaries, and Turkey has bankrolled the group to the tune of $300 million. Erdogan has taken his country "from NATO ally to terror sponsor."

There are, to be sure, marked differences between Turkey and Egypt, a particular focus of the book, but the Islamists in both countries are working from the same playbook:

- Profess anodyne goals initially, then gradually ratchet up to full-bore Islamist objectives? Check. In Egypt, the Muslim Brotherhood began by promising to contest fewer than 50 percent of the parliamentary seats—then contested nearly 80 percent; it promised not to field a presidential candidate—but eventually did so and handily installed a dyed-in-the-wool Islamist, Mohamed Morsi. Morsi had campaigned to ensure that Egypt's fundamental law would reflect "the sharia, then the sharia, and finally, the sharia."

- Roll out enforcement of sharia norms in daily life? Check. During Ramadan, a religious edict was announced prohibiting Egyptians from eating during daylight hours.
- Openly turn away from America, Israel, the West to embrace the jihadist agenda? Check. The Brotherhood's Supreme Guide issued a call for jihad until "the filth of the Zionists" is cleansed and "Muslim rule throughout our beloved Palestine" is imposed.

McCarthy carefully delimits the scope of his predictive analysis. The Islamization of Turkey was slowed by the military, the designated guardian of the country's explicitly secular character. Egypt, by contrast, has never undergone an enforced secularization campaign, nor is the military's role predictable. (Having published the book well before the military ousting of Morsi, presumably McCarthy would regard the ensuing pro-Morsi demonstrations as evidence of an enduring, potent constituency for Islamist rule.) And the endgame in Egypt appears far off.

The significance of McCarthy's argument is broader than the rise of Islamists in Turkey, post-Mubarak Egypt, and elsewhere. The very notion of "Islamic democracy," he argues, is a dangerous misconception—one that the West fuels and Islamists exploit. Western leaders and intellectuals, he maintains, have failed (some refuse) to grasp the nature and popularity of the Islamist movement, and by advocating "democracy" in the Middle East have encouraged and materially enabled forces hostile to the West.

Islamists, McCarthy ably explains, should be defined not by their tactics but by their animating goal of enforcing rule under the supreme dictates of sharia. Some adopt violent, terrorist means, others the genteel Western forms of political campaigning and advocacy, but their objectives are identical. And McCarthy plausibly contends that in the culture of the Muslim Middle East, obedience to political authority and the totalitarian interpretation of Islam are both well within the mainstream.

McCarthy holds that culture shapes politics and law, and that elections merely reflect popular sentiment. The authentic, Western idea of "democracy," in McCarthy's view, is gutted of its substantive meaning when applied to Islamic politics. More than "just elections and constitution-writing," democracy should be understood as a "shorthand description of a culture based on freedom." But Islamists, he complains, view "democracy" as a "mere vehicle, a procedural path of least resistance" toward a theocratic society bereft of individual freedoms. So, when a culture has been methodically inculcated with the teachings of Islamic totalitarianism, by the likes of the Muslim Brotherhood—when many in the culture have been taught to equate secular government with impiety, and when individual rights are unknown, and controversial speech is deemed blasphemous—what other result could possibly be expected at the ballot box?

The culture-comes-first argument is cogent, but McCarthy's redefinition of "democracy" as identical with the culture of a free society is unconvincing. Perhaps colloquial usage agrees with him, and certainly "democracy" evokes upbeat connotations, but America's founders would be aghast. They knew, from historical evidence and careful reflection, that the essence of democracy is mob rule, and that a government dedicated to protecting individual rights must never submit individual liberties to a popular vote. Unfortunately, recent American policy has arguably encouraged Islamists to embrace the actual meaning of democracy. President George W. Bush told reporters in 2004 that if Iraq, post-Saddam Hussein, were to vote in an Islamist government, he would be disappointed, but "democracy is democracy" adding, "If that's what the people choose, that's what the people choose." McCarthy's point would be better served by framing the issue in clearer terms.

"Where Bush airbrushed Islamic supremacists, Obama embraces them," writes McCarthy, and he goes on to expose how Obama has whitewashed and abetted the Muslim Brotherhood-backed regime that emerged post-Mubarak. But in view of the book's core argument, McCarthy is incongruously lenient toward Bush. When it was crucial to name precisely the nature and goals of the enemy, President Bush proffered designations (evil-doers, hijackers of a great religion, etc.) that deliberately obscured the identity of the Islamist movement, piling confusion upon the public's ignorance. And, considering Bush's signature policy of spreading democracy, it is hard to imagine a figure who did more to prepare the ground for the "spring fever" self-delusion, the view that McCarthy so skillfully demolishes in this book. The reluctance to reach a more critical verdict is a peculiar omission in an otherwise trenchant analysis.

Hard-headed and richly detailed, *Spring Fever* lays bare the facts and trend lines behind the chilling ascendancy of Islamists.

What Happened to Egypt's "Arab Spring"?

Elan Journo June 9, 2014

Just over three years ago, Egypt was ruled by Hosni Mubarak's autocratic police-state. During the "Arab Spring," crowds massed in Tahrir Square to protest the Mubarak regime, and he was soon removed from his throne. Then Mohamed Morsi, aligned with the Islamist Muslim Brotherhood, took power. He sought to establish his own kind of tyrannical control. The military toppled him. Now, a new military-backed strongman, Abdel Fattah al-Sisi, heads Egypt. The country seems poised for another Mubarak-esque period. Egypt has swung from one kind of tyranny (dictatorship) to another (Islamist rule)—and back again. Why?

By way of answering that, I'd single out two salient factors. First, the military establishment and the Islamist factions are deeply entrenched, and in effect dominate the political scene. The military wields enormous control over the apparatus of the state. The religious groups, able to couch their positions in moral terms, can set the terms of debate. One result is that the few secular-oriented groups seeking some modicum of freedom are easily marginalized (see "Understanding the 'Arab Spring,'" p. 93). So the prospects for fundamental change—an enormous undertaking that would require many years—were dismal. A second factor is related to that: the better elements among the protesters in Tahrir Square were hamstrung by lacking a well-defined, positive ideological vision. You can see that point emerge in a riveting, poignant documentary, *The Square*. (The film can be watched on Netflix, and it's definitely worthwhile.)

The film tracks a politically diverse group of friends united by outrage, standing together in the massive protests at Tahrir Square. What lends the film its narrative power is that it enables us to listen to them, uncensored by the state. For example, we sit next to them in the living room of an apartment where the friends gather to track the news and make plans and to argue. The fall of Mubarak fills them with elation, the subsequent rise of the Muslim Brotherhood, gloom. When the military reasserts control in summer 2013—opening fire on crowds with live ammunition and mowing down protestors with armored vans—the sheer brutality is overwhelming.

Dejected and pensive, one of the protesters in the film reflects on the turmoil. Thinking out loud as much as addressing the documentary crew, he points out that the protesters were united against the Mubarak regime, and that enabled them to bring together many different factions at the Square—but what, exactly, were they for? Without that, he muses, how far could they get.

PART 4

The Islamist Cause: Undefeated, Emboldened, Marching On

Draw Muhammad, Risk Your Life?

Elan Journo   October 6, 2010

Molly Norris was a cartoonist for the *Seattle Weekly*, and although she's still alive, she's gone "ghost": leaving her job, moving, changing her name, and essentially erasing any traces of her identity. For fear of her life.

Exercising her right to free speech—and encouraging others to do the same—she promoted "Everybody Draw Muhammed Day." In July, the Islamist cleric Anwar al-Awlaki (who's linked to the Times Square bomber) announced that Norris "should be taken as a prime target of assassination."(!) Now, at the insistence of the FBI, Norris has gone into the equivalent of a witness protection program—on her own dime.

This scandal has been unfolding for a while . . . so where are the outraged, fire-breathing editorials in our leading newspapers? Where are the impassioned speeches from politicians upholding the inalienable right of Americans to freedom of speech—and specifically, our right to criticize and ridicule ideologies of every stripe? The muted response to Norris's fate, the lack of outrage—particularly from the news media—is horrifying. That our political leaders have pointedly shied away from taking a stand on this is all the more ominous. Government's crucial job is to protect our rights.

Have we sunk so low that drawing Muhammad means risking your life? Is America willing to surrender the fundamental right to freedom of speech in obedience to the dictates of some Islamist cleric?

Jihadist in the Suburbs

Elan Journo   October 19, 2010

The headlines can be macabre—"Make a Bomb in the Kitchen of Your Mom"—and the stories (giving advice on how to pack when you leave for jihad) are in colloquial English. *Inspire* magazine is the work of al-Qaeda's affiliate in Yemen. But the editor behind this publication—which has encouraged would-be jihadists to open fire on lunch crowds in D.C., to take out some U.S. government employees—is a Pakistani-American. NPR has a long, unsettling report on that 24-year-old man, Samir Khan.

One point that caught my eye: while still living in his parents' basement, here in the U.S., Khan published a pro-al-Qaeda website—but took pains, even hiring a lawyer to advise him, so as not to run afoul of the law. Someone who knew him tells NPR that that step defied Khan's Islamist creed. "For him to take shade under the Constitution or to go to a disbelieving lawyer and ask for his help contradicts the entire ideological worldview that he has decided to live by."

Really? Islamic totalitarian groups like Hamas have stooped to taking part in representative elections for government power—as a means of advancing their dictatorial agenda. Ditto for Hezbollah. Islamists have shown in the past that they're quite happy to work "within the system" in order to subvert it. In Europe, there are Islamist activists who use lawful means—lobbying, special pleading, lawsuits—to impose their ideology on others. I touch on this topic in my book, *Winning the Unwinable War*. The point here: it's a myth that Islamists use only the tactic of terrorism in pursuit of their ideological goal—far from it.

Freedom of Speech, "Islamophobia," and the Cartoons Crisis

Elan Journo   December 18, 2014

Excerpts from an interview with Flemming Rose, author of
The Tyranny of Silence

Is there a climate of self-censorship regarding Islam? Has fear led artists and writers to avoid discussion and criticism of Islam? So it seemed to the journalists at *Jyllands-Posten*, Denmark's largest daily paper, in the fall of 2005. To assess the situation, the newspaper invited artists to submit cartoons about Islam. The reaction to the twelve cartoons that were published? Protests, boycotts, deadly riots, attacks on Danish embassies. Some 200 people are thought to have died in the protests. The "cartoons crisis" had gone global.

The aftershocks continued. Just two examples: Yale University Press decided to cut every image depicting Muhammad from a new scholarly book analyzing the cartoons crisis. Kurt Westergaard, the Danish cartoonist who depicted Muhammad with a bomb in his turban, was driven into hiding, escaping two attempts on his life.

What is the situation like today? That was one of the questions I put to Flemming Rose, the editor who commissioned and published the cartoons. He has written a perceptive and riveting new book about the crisis, the reaction to it, and the future of free speech. The book's title hints at the direction of the current trend: *The Tyranny of Silence: How One Cartoon Ignited a Global Debate on the Future of Free Speech*.

Our conversation ranged widely. A few of the issues we touched on: what incidents prompted the commissioning of the cartoons, how self-censorship operated under the Soviet regime and the parallels to today, what lies behind the push to outlaw "defamation of religion," and why the invalid term "Islamophobia" is so destructive.

Below is an excerpt from that interview, edited for inclusion in this book. You can listen to the entire interview (and download the MP3) on our website: bit.ly/tyranny-of-silence.

Elan Journo: *I'm delighted to be speaking today with Flemming Rose about his new book* The Tyranny of Silence: How One Cartoon Ignited a Global Debate on the Future of Free Speech. *Welcome to the podcast.*

Flemming Rose: It's really a pleasure.

EJ: *What led you to commission the cartoons and then to decide to publish them?*

FR: Some people think that these cartoons came out of the blue, that we just decided to publish some cartoons depicting the prophet, to make a statement or to provoke somebody or because of other reasons. But in fact they didn't come out of the blue. They were published as a reaction to a sequence of incidents in Denmark, beginning in the middle of September 2005.

At the time a children's author went public, saying, 'I'm writing a book about the life of the prophet Muhammad, but I have problems finding an illustrator.' Two illustrators had turned down the offer to illustrate the book. Finally, one illustrator said yes, but insisted on anonymity, due to fear for possible consequences. When an artist doesn't want to publish something in his own name, that's a form of self-censorship.

The story was on the front page of my newspaper, and several other newspapers. Following up on the story, we had a discussion at my newspaper. One reporter suggested that we find out if there really was self-censorship among people working in the field of culture in Denmark: The idea was to approach illustrators and cartoonists, and ask them to draw the prophet to see how they react. That idea ended on my desk, and so I wrote a letter to all the members of Denmark's cartoonist association inviting them to draw the prophet as they see him—a very open invitation, and that's the reason why in fact the cartoons are so different. I received twelve cartoons.

EJ: *How many people did you approach?*

FR: I approached, in fact, forty-two people. But I was told in the middle of the process that, in fact, there were only twenty-five active members of the illustrators' association, so about 50 percent replied. At the newspaper, we had a discussion about whether this was enough in order to go on with the project. But when I was told that it was about 50 percent, we thought that it's fine. But we put off publishing the cartoons for about another two weeks, because we had just this one source to this story—the children's writer who said that he couldn't find an illustrator.

While we were discussing those issues at the newspaper, several things happened that convinced me and the other editors that we had to publish those cartoons.

First, the illustrator who had originally insisted on anonymity gave an interview to a Danish newspaper. He acknowledged in public that it was true that he insisted on anonymity because he was afraid. He referred to the fate of Theo van Gogh, a Dutch filmmaker, who was killed on the streets of Amsterdam by a young, offended Muslim in November 2004. The illustrator also referred to the fate of Salman Rushdie, the author of *Satanic Verses*, who was subjected to a fatwa by Ayatollah Khamenei, and had to live in hiding for many.

Then, at the Tate gallery, an art museum in London, there was a retrospective by a very famous British avant-garde artist, John Latham. He exhibited an installation called *God is Great*. It's a copy of the Bible, Talmud, and the Koran torn into pieces and laid in a piece of glass. The Tate museum decided to remove this piece of art from the exhibition without asking the artist and without asking the curator. There was a similar case at a museum in Sweden, where an artist exhibited a painting depicting a man and a woman having sex, and on the top of the painting was the first verse from the Koran. Again, the director of the museum removed this painting, without asking the artist or the curator.

Another example of self-censorship related to a book by Ayaan Hirsi Ali, a former Dutch politician now residing in the U.S. She had written a collection of essays critical of Islam. Without consulting her, the publisher of the Finnish edition of the book removed a sentence that was seen as maybe offensive to Muslims. Also: several of the European translators of the book insisted on anonymity. Contrary to the usual practice, they did not want to have their name published on the cover or inside the book.

Yet another incident: A Danish stand-up comedian gave an interview to my newspaper in which he said, "you know, I have no problems mocking the Bible in front of the camera, but I'm afraid of doing the same with the Koran." So he was making a clear difference between the way he would treat Christianity when it comes to satire, and the way he would treat Islam.

And then the prime minister of Denmark met with a group of Danish imams. This was in the aftermath of the London bombings of July 7, 2005. Two of the imams called on him to influence the Danish press in order to get more positive coverage of Islam, which was basically a call for censorship. It was a call to use the tools of state power in order to get a specific point of view into the press. Both of the imams said this in public after the meeting.

So within the course of one or two weeks, you had several cases all speaking to the same problem of self-censorship when it comes to dealing with Islam in the public space in Denmark and in some other European countries. So we decided that this is a legitimate news story.

You know, in journalism you hear about a problem, and then you want to find out if it's true or not. Usually you would call people and they will tell you what they think about this and that. We just pursued another path, basically following a classic journalistic principle, "Don't tell, show it." So [in writing to the Danish illustrators] we had invited them to show through the medium in which they work to express their opinion, their relationship to this problem.

[Alongside the twelve cartoons we published,] I wrote a short article laying out the background, referring to what I knew about the Soviet Union—that you could end up in prison for ten years for telling a joke in Stalin's Soviet Union—and that this kind of intimidation leads to self-censorship and it's a slippery slope. In this case, we didn't know for sure if this was true or not.

But the events that followed, I think, showed that we really hit a hotspot.

To listen to the entire interview (and download the MP3), please visit ARI's website: bit.ly/tyranny-of-silence.

Freedom of Speech: We Will Not Cower

Onkar Ghate   January 7, 2015

When foreign governments, religious leaders and their faithful followers threaten and murder individuals for daring to speak, anyone who values his own life and freedom must stand with, and speak for, the victims.

We call on everyone to post and publicize the content that these totalitarians do not want us to see, as we are doing here.

It does not matter whether you agree or disagree with the particular book, cartoon or movie that they seek to silence. We must defend our unconditional right to freedom of thought and freedom of speech.

The totalitarians are counting on self-censorship: that their threats and attacks will leave most of us too scared to speak out and criticize their doctrines. They then have a chance of killing the few individuals brave enough to defy them.

We must end any hope that this strategy will prove effective.

In the wake of the attacks on Sony, many people rightly observed that if *The Interview* were put up on the Internet and made widely available, the attackers' goal of silencing the filmmaker would be unachieved. The same goes for criticism and satire of Islamic doctrine.

If we now all defiantly make the content and images the jihadists wish to ban widely and permanently available across the web, the attackers will have failed. They may have taken the lives of the editor and cartoonists of *Charlie Hebdo*, for which we grieve, but they will not have taken their freedom.

The alternative is to cower and stick our heads in the sand in hope that the issue goes away. But this will not end the threat. It will only make our freedom disappear.

#JeSuisCharlie . . . But for How Long?

Elan Journo January 12, 2015

The aftermath of the *Charlie Hebdo* attack has brought an encouraging reaction. You can see it on the streets of Paris and other cities. Last week, tens of thousands of people joined vigils in solidarity for the murdered journalists. Upwards of a million Parisians took to the streets on Sunday. "Je Suis Charlie" read the signs. Online the corresponding hashtag has swept across social media. Some news outlets—more than I expected—have reprinted *Charlie Hebdo* cartoons. But what's more, the outlets that have refused to publish the images (or pixelated them) have been deservedly bashed. They shame themselves by cowering.

We are all Charlie—at least today and next week. But what happens once grief and horror naturally attenuate over time?

For the Je Suis Charlie phenomenon to translate into a strengthening of freedom of speech, a great deal depends on the conclusions people form and act on going forward.

Jeffrey Goldberg at *The Atlantic* admonishes that few fully appreciate what it means to stand up for freedom of speech, or have the courage to do so themselves. I'd add: where was the solidarity nearly a decade ago for *Jyllands-Posten*, Flemming Rose, and the artists who were driven in to hiding after the Muhammad cartoons crisis? And before that, after the murder of filmmaker Theo van Gogh? Or, for *Charlie Hebdo* in 2011 when its offices were firebombed?

By now people have many, many more data points. Now, as in the past, the pattern is blatant. The jihadists seek to extinguish the freedom of speech. At *Charlie Hebdo*, the killers declared that they were avenging the prophet. They voiced a standard battle cry, "Allahu Akbar." They executed the journalists during an editorial meeting.

The future will bring continuing assaults on the freedom of speech. The courage to defend that freedom presupposes a real understanding of it. What's vital now is to champion the freedom of speech, to inform and educate all who will listen. If you value your life and freedom, you should speak up in whatever forum is open to you. Join ARI in our effort to defend the irreplaceable right to the freedom of speech.

Learn about ARI's uncompromising defense of freedom of speech: AynRand.org/freespeech.

Free Speech vs. Religion:
An Interview with Onkar Ghate

The Undercurrent June 23, 2015

Onkar Ghate is a senior fellow and the Chief Content Officer at the Ayn Rand Institute. He has written and lectured extensively on philosophy and serves as dean for the Institute's Objectivist Academic Center in Irvine, California. *The Undercurrent's* Jon Glatfelter had the privilege of interviewing Ghate regarding the May 3, 2015, shooting at the Draw Muhammad cartoon contest in Garland, Texas, as well as religion and free speech, more broadly.

The Undercurrent: *Many of the major U.S. media players, including CNN and FOX, still have not published the cartoon contest's winning piece. Why do you think that is?*

Onkar Ghate: I haven't kept tabs on which outlets have and have not published that cartoon, but there were similar responses in regard to the *Charlie Hebdo* cartoons and, before that, the Danish cartoons in 2005–06. Sometimes a media outlet would try to explain why it is not showing its audience a crucial element of the news story, and I think these explanations have revealed a mixture of motives at work.

Here's a non-exhaustive list: fear, cowardice, appeasement, sympathy. Let me say a word on each. Some media outlets are afraid of violent reprisals and of the ongoing security costs that would be necessary to protect staff. And because the U.S. government refuses to take an unequivocal stand in defense of the right to free speech, the totalitarians are emboldened, which makes violent reprisals more likely. So that's one reason. But despite this legitimate fear, I do think there is often an element of cowardice. The likelihood of an attack can be overstated, and of course if more news outlets publish the cartoons, it is more and more difficult to intimidate and attack them all, and less and less likely that a particular organization will be singled out. Here there is strength in numbers. A third motive is the appeaser's false hope that if he gives in and doesn't publish the cartoons, he will have satisfied the attackers and no further threats or demands will follow. Finally, many are sympathetic: out of deference to the non-rational, faith-based emotions of Muslims, they don't publish the cartoons, even though those cartoons are news. They view the cartoonists and publishers as the troublemakers and villains. (The roots of this sympathy, I think, are complex and often ugly.)

TU: *Some have condemned the contest's organizer, Pamela Geller, and the winning artist, Bosch Fawstin. They say there's a world of difference between good-natured free expression and malicious speech intended solely to antagonize. What do you think?*

OG: I disagree with many things that I've heard Pamela Gellar say, but I refuse to discuss her real or alleged flaws when totalitarians are trying to kill her, as though those flaws, even if real, justify or mitigate the actions of the aspiring killers. The *New York Times* editorial to which you link is a disgrace. After a sanctimonious paragraph saying that we all have the right to publish offensive material and that no matter how offensive that material may be, it does not justify murder, the rest of the editorial goes on to criticize the victim of attempted murder. As my colleague and others have noted, this is like denouncing a rape victim instead of her rapists.

And notice what the editorial glosses over: in the first paragraph stating that offensive material does not justify murder, it concludes with the seemingly innocuous point that "it is incumbent on leaders of all religious faiths to make this clear to their followers."

This is the actual issue. Why don't you similarly have to tell a group of biochemists or historians, when they disagree about a theory, that their disagreements don't justify murdering each other? The answer lies in the difference between reason and faith, as I'm sure we'll discuss, a difference the editorial dares not discuss.

But contra the editorial, the Garland event had a serious purpose. Look at the winning cartoon: it makes a serious point.

Whether we will admit it or not, there exists today a growing number of totalitarians who seek to impose their version of Islam on the world and to dictate what we in the West can and cannot say. A precedent-setting episode was the fatwah against Salman Rushdie. A foreign leader openly calls for the assassination of a Western author and those involved in the publishing of his book, *The Satanic Verses*, and the U.S. and other Western governments do virtually nothing in response, sometimes worse than nothing.

Fast forward a few years and should it be surprising that there exists a climate of self-censorship with respect to Islam? Western writers, artists and cartoonists are afraid to publish things that might be deemed blasphemous by Muslims. To investigate the extent of the self-censorship in regard to illustrations of Muhammad, the Danish newspaper *Jyllands-Posten* runs a cartoon contest in 2005. Worldwide riots and outrage ensue, death threats proliferate, cartoonists and newspaper editors go into hiding, some are later attacked, and the official Western response to all this is again mostly pathetic.

To me this is a serious problem. There are many other episodes that could be mentioned to drive home the extent of the problem, but a simple way to appreciate its extent is to ask yourself whether you can imagine that instead of the sacrilegious *Book of Mormon* winning over audiences and critics on Broadway, it is the equally sacrilegious musical "The Koran." Right now, this isn't even in the realm of the possible. Remember what happened when, in the face of the Danish cartoons crisis, Trey Parker and Matt Stone tried to depict Muhammad on *South Park*?

Now in the face of a totalitarian movement that commands us not to utter blasphemous thoughts and threatens us with death if we do, coupled with our own government's appeasing responses, I think it becomes the responsibility of any self-respecting citizen to refuse to cower and for us as a culture to refuse to collapse into self-censorship. Instead, proudly and defiantly utter the blasphemous thoughts. I think a worthy project during the Rushdie years would have been to raise a fund to make his life in hiding easier, purchase the rights to his book for a generous sum, and then publish and distribute millions of copies for free. Similarly with the *Charlie Hebdo* assassinations, I argued that the forbidden cartoons should be plastered all over the Internet. Let it be seen that the attempt to ban these works achieves the opposite. Make it clear that the totalitarians' goal requires killing us all. Declare that I, too, am Spartacus.

I view the Fawstin cartoon as in this same spirit and thus as making a serious, needed point.

TU: *I have friends who want to stand up for free speech but are worried about being labeled "intolerant" by their friends and acquaintances. How do you think everyday citizens should act?*

OG: I've already indicated part of my answer. The totalitarians' goal is to silence us and make us obey. The current tactic is assassination of those who dare speak. The hope is that these attacks will create enough fear to produce widespread self-censorship.

Unfortunately, that hope is materializing. Defy them. Put up on your Facebook or Instagram pages the forbidden cartoons and explain that you are purposely doing so in the name of free speech and in order to combat the climate of self-censorship. Or put up links to places that do this, such as ARI.

More generally, among some of the best people today in the West, there is a frightening lack of understanding of the right to free speech, why it is vital, who its enemies are at home and abroad, past and present. Educate yourself about this crucial right and its history, and then try to convince your friends and acquaintances of the importance of the issue.

If you get called names in the process, try to use this as a conversation starter and don't become defensive. Ask the person what he means by "intolerance" and if he can state his actual position. Is his view that we should obey every religious taboo? Many Hindus regard cows as sacred and find it offensive that we eat beef. Should we stop eating beef out of tolerance or respect? Or should we stop doing so only if a group of organized Hindus starts assassinating chefs at steakhouses? Won't this encourage religionists to use violence? Or perhaps his view is that we should not criticize religion? Why not? And does he apply this to all religions, or just Islam? If just Islam, why does it warrant special status?

So my advice is that if you are truly talking about friends and acquaintances with whom you have a positive relationship, treat them as open to persuasion even if they begin by dismissing or belittling your position, politely stand your ground, and discuss and argue.

But of course this presupposes that you have some understanding of the issues involved.

TU: *In a recent panel with Flemming Rose, author of The Tyranny of Silence, you said that an individual's right to free speech is one application of a more fundamental right: the right to think. Could you explain that?*

OG: The great battle for freedom in the West was a battle for freedom of thought, including everything this freedom presupposes and everything it leads to. The right to freedom of thought is the right to think for yourself, which means the right to engage in a reasoning process: to gather evidence, logically analyze and weigh it, entertain different arguments, form and follow hypotheses, perform experiments, pursue various lines of questioning, etc., etc. A reasoning process can have no master other than facts and logic. It cannot be subordinate to the approval of a king, pope, president or fellow citizen, no matter how much they disagree or are offended by what you think. An aspect of this process is to be able to freely discuss and debate ideas with others, and to then present your views and conclusions in an effort to persuade others. Freedom of thought and freedom of speech go together.

Historically, the opponents of freedom of thought and freedom of speech are political authorities operating with the sanction of religion (or some other mystical dogma, like Marxism or Nazism) and religious leaders wielding political power.

TU: *If you view faith and force as intimately linked phenomena, do you see reason and freedom as linked? If so, how has the United States, with its largely Judeo-Christian culture, remained arguably more free than less religious parts of Europe?*

OG: Yes, the connection between faith and force and between reason and freedom is a philosophical issue that some thinkers in the Enlightenment made great strides in identifying and that I think Ayn Rand fully explains.

Very briefly, to extol faith is to extol, in thought and action, blind submission and obedience. As a natural consequence, force will be seen as a means of achieving the good: you can make someone blindly submit and obey by threatening to burn him at the stake or to chop his head off.

But what you cannot achieve by the instruments of terror is rational understanding, knowledge, enlightenment. These require that a person himself initiate and direct a process of reason. And this means that if the goal is rational understanding and knowledge, the individual must have the freedom to think and speak. This is why the Age of Enlightenment became the champion of these freedoms.

To answer the second part of the question, the U.S. is not a Judeo-Christian nation. It is the first nation to consciously separate church from state. It is the last, great accomplishment of the Age of Enlightenment and is built on the Greek-Roman achievements that began to be rediscovered during the Renaissance. Nor is it true that Europe is less faith-based than is America. Yes, Americans are overall more overtly religious, but the faith-based doctrines of nationalism, fascism, socialism and communism swept across Europe in a way that they never did in the U.S. Since the time of the American Revolution and its grounding in the Age of Enlightenment, culturally both Europe and America have moved in the direction of mysticism, but Europe has been more mystical than the U.S. and consequently less free.

For a fuller discussion of these issues, you can watch my talks "Religion vs. Freedom" and "The Morality of Freedom."

TU: In his recent interview with The Undercurrent, *Bosch Fawstin labeled himself "anti-Islam." He described Islam as a fundamentally "totalitarian ideology." Is it different from other religions in this respect?*

OG: There is, in essence, no difference. Any mystical, faith-based doctrine whose leaders are trying to usurp the role of a rational philosophy in human life—as Christians did during the Greek-Roman period, as socialist-Marxists and fascist-Nazis did during the 19th and 20th centuries, and as Islamists are trying to do today—is dictatorial and becomes totalitarian.

Each of these movements is seeking blind submission and obedience to a comprehensive worldview. It should come as no surprise that the daily submission and obedience they desire will eventually be enforced at gunpoint.

This is true of ISIS, of the theocrats in Iran and Saudi Arabia, of the Taliban, of the communists in Russia and China, of Protestants like Calvin and Martin Luther, and of leaders of the Catholic Church.

TU: A widely held view is that Islam, to say nothing of the world's other major religions, is peaceful. In fact, immediately post-9/11, President George W. Bush described Islam as a religion "of peace" that has been "hijacked." Do you agree?

OG: Like much of what comes out of George W. Bush's mouth, this is the opposite of the truth. As I've already indicated, the essence of religion, namely faith, sanctions the use of force. If blind submission and obedience are the goals, coercion is an effective means. A worldview accepted on faith encourages not peace but war. Centuries of religious conflict and warfare are not some inexplicable accident.

Also no accident is that the greatest of America's founding fathers, Jefferson and Madison, deliberately separated church from state. They did so partly in the name of peace. Let us live under principles and laws whose origin is reason, not blind faith, and we can all rationally agree to them and live peacefully together.

TU: It seems that free expression is under assault on a number of fronts today. What does this issue of free speech mean to you personally? Why have you chosen to dedicate a significant portion of your scholarship to defending it?

OG: Because of their viewpoints, many of the Enlightenment's thinkers were on the run from the political and religious authorities. But they eventually won and put an end to such arbitrary power. It is an enormous accomplishment and an enormous gift, not to be surrendered.

I'm an intellectual. My entire career revolves around the reasoned investigation and communication of philosophical ideas and theories, ideas and theories that others often find offensive. If I won't stand up for my right to freedom of thought and speech, and fight for these, I have no business calling myself an intellectual. And I have no business professing admiration for Locke, Jefferson, Madison and other heroes of freedom, if I stand idly by as people try to smash their achievements.

TU: Do you have any recommendations for those who want to explore the topics of free speech and religion in more depth? Can we expect any future projects or events on these issues from you or the Institute?

OG: I've already mentioned a few things of mine and of others at ARI that people can read and watch. Flemming Rose's book, to which you linked, is also definitely worth reading. For those who don't know, he was the editor who published the Danish cartoons; I admire his benevolence and courage.

In a few weeks I will be speaking at OCON, where I will address some of these issues in more detail, including some issues that we did not have time to touch on today. The talk's titled *"Charlie Hebdo,* the West and the Need to Ridicule Religion." I hope to see some of your readers there!

And of course in the months and years to come, look to ARI to continue to uphold and defend the individual's right to freedom of thought and speech.

Iran Nuclear Deal:
The Diplomacy-or-War False Alternative

Elan Journo   July 23, 2015

When Obama announced the Iran nuclear deal, he explained the rationale for taking the diplomatic path. There were, he said, three options: negotiate as good a deal as we can get; pull out of the talks; or else take military action against Iran's nuclear facilities, igniting another Middle East war. Turns out these boil down to only two options, really, since pulling out of talks, according to Obama, would also end up leading to military action. So, if the options are diplomacy versus going to war, you can see why Obama's case has swayed some people. But that argument hinges on a tendentious framing of the possibilities.

Obama's either/or argument is a classic example of a false alternative. When the deal was announced, an editorial in the *Wall Street Journal* rightly protested that there was at least one more option: inflicting even stronger economic sanctions to pressure Iran. Fair point: Obama's two alternatives hardly exhaust the possibilities. In my view, the time for considering sanctions, with all of their limitations, passed long ago. But the point stands: Obama's argument hinges on an alternative that's unduly narrow.

Now look at how Obama's argument slants the framing of the two alternatives. Start with the administration's preferred option, a negotiated deal.

Advocates of the deal portray it as requiring inspections so "intrusive" that if the Iranians inched beyond the terms of the deal, "the world would know it." Except that the administration has already started walking back the hyped claim that nuclear inspectors will have "anytime, anyplace" access. The record on monitoring such nuclear deals is pitiful: recall that in 1994 the Clinton administration struck a deal with North Korea over its nuclear program. That deal subjected North Korea to strict nuclear inspections, but the regime has since built and tested nuclear devices and sold some of its technology.

Of course, Iran has cheated at every step so far. The question is not if, but when and in what way(s) Tehran will violate the deal. In theory Iran would face a "snap back" re-imposition of sanctions, if its breach of the deal could ever be detected and if the facts can be agreed upon by a multi-nation committee. Good luck with that.

To imagine that this alternative can reduce the threat of a nuclear Iran is ridiculous. It's like popping two Advil in the expectation of curing a fast-growing cancerous tumor. You delude yourself that you're "doing something" about the problem—Advil is a medicine, after all—even while allowing it to worsen.

The chief selling point for Obama's nuclear deal, however, lies in what the deal is not—it's not military force. And by that, he means we can avoid another Iraq.

The Iraq war was a debacle. And we all recoil from the idea of another quagmire. Is it right, though, to equate military force with a monumentally irrational, disastrous application of such power, the Iraq war? No.

The military is a powerful instrument, but it is our foreign policy that directs it. Clearly military force can be—and, in the past, has been—guided by better policy, and it was effective in advancing our self-defense (World War II comes to mind). What unfolded in Iraq was nothing like the military action necessary for our self-defense. In *Winning the Unwinnable War*, I explain that it was fundamentally a policy, not a military failure: in short, it was a nation-building welfare mission, not a self-interested mission to eliminate threats we faced. The wider point is that it's tendentious to equate the Iraq war (as horrific and disgraceful as it was) with military action in self-defense, and then dismiss that option.

The Iraq war should be taken as discrediting, not military action, but the ideas of our policymakers, who set the battle plans for the military.

What's missing from the debate over Iran is the one option we most need: a fundamentally different approach to our foreign policy, one that properly identifies and eliminates threats to our lives and freedom. For my detailed answer about how to respond to Iran, I point you to my book. Two brief points:

First, we have put ourselves into a situation with Iran that a rational foreign policy would never permit us to get into. We find ourselves here, precisely because Washington for years has followed a perversely short-range and unprincipled foreign policy. At the time of Iran's first act of war against us, three decades ago, we should have retaliated decisively. We didn't. We should have acted after Iran's second, third, fourth, umpteenth act of war. We didn't. For the last decade plus, the evidence of the regime's nuclear program was ineluctable, but we basically allowed it to proceed. For years by letting Iran attack us with impunity, we've encouraged it. By wooing it to the negotiating table—a process that began under Bush—we've signaled that we regard it as a legitimate interlocutor.

Second, we have disarmed ourselves even as the threat from Iran has grown. We ought to recognize that military action—from threats, ultimatums, targeted strikes, and up to war—is sometimes necessary to defend ourselves and (when guided by rational principles) effectual. I have argued that the threat from Iran requires applying military coercion in our self-defense. That would look far different from the self-destructive mission in Iraq. In chapter 7 of my book—which you can read here in PDF—I illustrate the sharp contrast between the policies that begat the nightmare of Iraq and what a rational approach entails.

One of the many pernicious consequences of Bush's foreign policy is that people have come to believe that our military—despite being unrivaled—is ineffectual and, if used, counter-productive. This notion that our self-defense must preclude military action goes a long way to explaining how Obama's nuclear deal is seen as even remotely plausible.

The Iran Nuclear Deal and the Split-Personality Fallacy

Elan Journo August 10, 2015

Why are seemingly sensible people cheering the Iran deal, given the regime's notorious brutality and belligerence? The answer lies in a wonkish affliction that you could call the split-personality fallacy.

Glance at the regime we're talking about. Iran is a horrific theocracy that methodically violates individual rights. Iran's worldwide backing of jihadists last year (according to our own government) was "undiminished." Across the Middle East, Iran vigorously seeks dominion: in Beirut, Damascus, Sanaa, Baghdad and Gaza, it already exerts significant influence, and it has begun outreach to the Taliban. Post-deal, might the mass chants in Iran of "Death to America" end? Might the regime's hostility toward us ("the Great Satan") abate? Whoever cherishes such hopes had them slapped down by Iran's "supreme leader" Ayatollah Khamenei: Our policy toward the "arrogant" U.S. government, he announced after the deal, "won't change at all."

And yet: in a major speech last week at American University, President Obama noted the deal's many backers:

> The United Nations Security Council has unanimously supported it. The majority of arms control and non-proliferation experts support it. Over 100 former ambassadors— who served under Republican and Democratic presidents— support it.

To that tally, add two scholars from the self-described libertarian Cato Institute, who also praised it. They argued that the "agreement must be viewed as a clear success."

How could anyone think that it's a good idea to negotiate with an openly hostile regime that fuels jihadists and seeks our destruction? Enter the split-personality fallacy. The crux of this fallacy is to treat the actions of Iran (or another tyranny we want to engage diplomatically) in isolation, as if carried out by distinct, firewalled personalities

---

This article originally appeared in *The Federalist*.

that happen to coexist in the same physical regime. Iran's drive for nuclear capability (officially: for civilian purposes!) reflects one personality. Iran's pervasive violation of individual rights domestically? That's another. How about its ongoing backing of jihadist groups? Still another. What about Iran's quest for regional domination? Yet another, dissociated personality.

The logic of this fractured perspective means that we must handle each personality separately, divorced from any wider context. Thus, many boosters of the Iran deal bless it on the minutely narrow grounds that it might delay Iran's nuclear program. Everything else— the domestic repression, the drive for regional conquest, the backing of jihadists, the hostility toward us—all of that's beyond the deal's scope, and therefore not something we should consider in judging the deal and consequences.

The segmenting out of Iran's nuclear program for piecemeal attention is touted as reflecting a nuanced, hard-headed concern with practicality. But what actually underlies the fractured, ultra-narrow approach toward Iran is a desire to evade the regime's animating ideological character. Observe how we have no concern about nuclear weapons in the hands of the UK or France; but precisely the same weapon in Iran's hands is a grave concern, because of its militant character. Push that out of mind, though, and you can dream up a deal-able-with persona, one which (like the UK or France) might actually comply with a pact.

But ignoring Iran's character is policy malpractice. To assess the situation rationally and formulate sound policy, it is crucial that we have a clear understanding of the regime's character. Is it a good idea to negotiate with Iran? Is the nuclear deal signed in Vienna a "clear success"? When you look at the contours of Iran's nature, you see that in truth the answers are: no, and no.

The Iranian regime embodies the idea of Islamic totalitarianism. Its founder and first "supreme leader," Ayatollah Khomeini, brought into reality a theory of clerical rule. Tehran demands from its citizens submission to religious law. Ergo the "morality police" that patrol the streets and harass women for wearing the wrong kind of veil. At the core is the totalitarian ambition to subjugate people. Witness the fate of six Iranian twenty-somethings who videoed themselves singing along to Pharrell's "Happy." Their video went viral. Then they were arrested, tried and found guilty of "participation in the making of a vulgar clip" and "illegitimate relations between members of the group."

They may yet escape being flogged or doing jail time (their sentence), but the fact that they were swept up for something so benign perfectly illustrates Tehran's rule-by-intimidation. Insulting the theocratic government and "blasphemy" are crimes. Hashem Shaabani, a poet, was accused of criticizing the regime. The executioner's noose wrung the life out of him. To the Iranian regime, human life is cheap.

This same totalitarian lust for domestic subjugation animates Tehran's aggression beyond its borders. Iran's founding constitution states that the Army and the Revolutionary Guards Corps

> will be responsible not only for guarding and preserving the frontiers of the country, but also for fulfilling the ideological mission of jihad in God's way; that is, extending the sovereignty of God's law throughout the world (this is in accordance with the Koranic verse "Prepare against them whatever force you are able to muster, and strings of horses, striking fear into the enemy of God and your enemy, and others besides them" [8:60]).

Iran has made good on that mission by helping to build and train jihadist groups. Its main proxy force is Hezbollah ("the army of God"). It has carried out attacks from Beirut to Buenos Aries, and it has slaughtered American soldiers and diplomats in Lebanon and in Iraq. Despite being subjected to years of supposedly biting economic sanctions, Iran funneled billions of dollars to support the Assad regime in Syria and to provision Hamas, in the Gaza strip, with weapons and rockets.

But suppose we took the facts of Iran's character seriously. We would be able to formulate a rational approach toward that regime. Here are two key takeaways that ought to shape it.

First, Iran's domestic repression and its imperialist march and its nuclear aspiration are inseparable. They stem from the same causal factor, the regime's declared ideological mission. If Allah's word is the Truth, and Iran's leaders definitely think so, then all mankind must be brought under its purview. How can there be any limits to where the Truth must reign? (Tehran certainly sees no such limits.) How can any means to advance that grandiose vision be precluded? (For Iran, none should be.) Going nuclear would provide Iran with a new means to advance the goal of expanding Allah's dominion.

Second, diplomatic engagement with Iran over the nuclear issue is a disaster in the making. Quite apart from the material "carrots" Iran might pocket and use to fund its jihadist proxies, simply allowing it to pull up a seat at the negotiating table is to confer on the regime an undeserved legitimacy. It implies that Iran, despite all the blood on its hands, is somehow a peace-seeking state; that despite its manifest belligerence, Iran is somehow committed to persuasion. Recall that Iran has engaged in deception at every step; here we're providing that tyranny with moral cover. Far from putting distance between Iran and the bomb, all that this appeasing deal can do is encourage the regime in its malignant campaign.

The split-personality fallacy sabotages policy thinking. Fracturing Iran's character into dissociated shards will not make Iran's character something other than what it clearly is. Blinding ourselves to it just puts great distance between us and the crucial facts needed to resolve the situation. And the nuclear deal promises to land us in graver problems down the road. It strengthens Iran, bringing the regime ever closer to going nuclear. By allowing that to happen, we will multiply the difficulty of using military force to defend ourselves from the Iranian menace. The reality we face is unpleasant and deeply distressing, but ignoring the truth can only subvert our security.

Cheering for the *Charlie Hebdo* Attacks: The Shape of Things to Come?

Elan Journo October 6, 2015

Ten years ago last week, the Danish newspaper *Jyllands-Posten* published twelve cartoons related to Islam. The aim was to gauge a seemingly growing climate of self-censorship in Europe. The ensuing crisis went global.

By looking at the erosion of free speech in Europe, you could see markers of what to expect here. European self-censorship, my colleague Onkar Ghate argued at the time, was coming to America. By the spring of 2006, Borders Books and Waldenbooks announced that they would not stock an upcoming issue of *Free Inquiry* magazine, because it reprinted some of the notorious cartoons.

The fear was pervasive. Major American news outlets refused to reprint the cartoons, even in reports on the rioting and deaths related to the cartoons crisis. Some years later, Yale University Press published a scholarly book analyzing the cartoons crisis—but decided just before going to press to excise every one of the twelve cartoons, along with other images.

In Europe, filmmakers, artists and writers had been threatened, attacked, murdered. Such threats and attacks were occurring here too.

In January 2015: Islamist gunmen massacred journalists at the magazine *Charlie Hebdo* in Paris. In May 2015: Islamists tried to attack a free speech event in Garland, Texas. Writing on *Voices for Reason*, Steve Simpson pointed out that the destruction of freedom of speech succeeds in large part because of the continuing appeasement in the West of those who resort to threats and violence. Steve's post, incidentally, was published five days before the Garland attack.

Although Europe is farther along, the trend is clear. That's what came to mind when I read Brendan O'Neill's account of a debate at the prestigious Trinity College, Dublin, in Ireland, on the right to be offensive. He writes:

> I was on the side of people having the right to say whatever the hell they want, no matter whose panties it bunches. The man on the other side who implied that *Charlie Hebdo* got what it deserved, and that the right to offend is a poi-

sonous, dangerous notion, was one Asghar Bukhari of the Muslim Public Affairs Committee.

It is depressing, but not surprising, that Bukhari's view is taken seriously. What I found bone-chilling is the reaction of students in the audience. They listened intently to Bukhari's case. Some cheered.

> This is how screwed-up the culture on Western campuses has become [writes O'Neill]: I was jeered for suggesting we shouldn't ban pop songs; Bukhari was cheered for suggesting journalists who mock Muhammad cannot be surprised if someone later blows their heads off.

One audience at one debate at one university in one city: obviously that's at most a data point, not a trend. But do the attitudes of these students—whom O'Neill describes as non-fringe, young and with-it—reflect broader trends in Europe? Quite possibly.

What does that imply for the future of free speech in Europe—and here?

San Bernardino and the Metastasizing Jihad

Elan Journo December 8, 2015

From the *Wall Street Journal*, on the butchers who carried out last week's attack in San Bernardino:

> Agents are pursuing "the very real possibility" that Ms. Malik was the catalyst for the violence, said one official. So far her husband "seems like someone who was searching for answers," the official said. . . .
>
> *An initial review of the couple's online activity indicates one or both explored propaganda from al-Qaeda and the Nusra Front, a terror group fighting in Syria,* officials said.
>
> *They also appear to have learned some terrorism tradecraft,* with investigators pointing to their move to smash their cellphones, stockpile thousands of rounds of ammunition and build more than a dozen black-powder pipe bombs.

From my book, *Winning the Unwinnable War: America's Self-Crippled Response to Islamic Totalitarianism* (Lexington Books, 2009):

> Suicide bombing, another tactic heavily practiced in Iraq [during the insurgency], is now rampant in Afghanistan. *The sharing of "best practices" among jihadists is potentially unlimited in its scale and lethal impact. Although person-to-person training may be the traditional mode of transferring combat knowledge, the Web offers Islamists an inexpensive, worldwide communications platform. Through bulletin boards, online videos, and written manuals, they can recruit fighters to their cause and disseminate to them hard-won expertise in mass murder, to be deployed anywhere.*
>
> Nothing that the United States has done in Iraq or Afghanistan has given jihadists reason to abandon their desire for such mass-casualty attacks on the West. Washington's policy has in fact left them stronger than before. *It has made the ideal of Islamic totalitarianism seem ever more viable—both by empowering and blessing Islamist rule, and by betraying its own timidity in the refusal to crush the jihad.*

This blog post originally appeared in *The Times of Israel.*

The Islamist equation that fidelity to Islam is the path to existential dominance, while American secularism (read: impiety) means weakness, thus gains added plausibility in their minds.

Emphasis added.

The Other Islamic State, Our Ally

Elan Journo　December 19, 2015

Why has Ashraf Fayadh, a poet and artist, been sentenced to death? A court of law found him "guilty on five charges that included spreading atheism, threatening the morals of . . . society and having illicit relations with women": he has been branded an apostate, for which the penalty is death. Where did this happen?

Maybe Raqqa, the stronghold of ISIS? Good guess, but no; it happened in the Kingdom of Saudi Arabia. Nor, of course, was this horrifying sentence an outlier; on the contrary. By one reckoning, lately the Saudi courts have handed down the "highest recorded number of executions in the kingdom since 1995." Some notable recent cases of Saudi "justice" have included:

> the public flogging of a liberal blogger; a death sentence for a protester for offenses committed as a minor; and a sentence of 350 blows for a British man who was arrested with alcohol in his car. (The Briton was released this month after spending more than a year in prison, averting the threatened flogging.)

There are many differences between Saudi Arabia and ISIS. The first is a monarchy, the second believes itself a true "caliphate," or Islamist regime. Saudi Arabia carries out floggings and beheadings without splashy, macabre propaganda videos, unlike ISIS. Saudi Arabia spends hundreds of millions on religious schools and books advancing its strain of Islamic totalitarianism worldwide; ISIS operatives spend a lot of time leveraging social media. The Saudi regime purports to be a U.S. ally; ISIS is at war with the West. These and umpteen other differences are real. They are overwhelmed, however, by the deeper commonality: the shared commitment to the political supremacy of Islamic law, sharia.

That's a fundamental causal factor, from which a great many consequences follow. And that factor would have to inform any serious thinking about our policy toward Saudi Arabia. Yet that regime has enjoyed an underserved standing as our ally, for many years.

This blog post originally appeared in *The Times of Israel*.

President George W. Bush embraced the Saudi regime, even hosting a member of the ruling family at his ranch. President Obama has (literally) bowed in deference to the Saudi king, while viewing the regime as an ally. What explains our irrational approach to Saudi Arabia?

A significant part of the answer lies in a perverse mindset, which Ayn Rand characterized as being "concrete-bound." In foreign policy, that mindset sees only scattered dots, never the trend lines that unite them (such as the decades-long ascent of Islamic totalitarianism across the Middle East); it sees discrete unrelated crises, not a sustained campaign (such as the escalating spiral of jihadist attacks in the years prior to 9/11); it sees only particular superficial features of regimes and Islamist factions, discounting the unifying role of their philosophic ideas (which animate the Islamist movement's diverse factions and state-sponsors). What this fractured mindset avoids is the integration of data into a conceptual perspective. And so, the essential similarity in ideology between Saudi Arabia and ISIS is left unseen, and it is purposely disregarded when inconvenient facts—like a death sentence for a poet—unavoidably intrude.

Ignoring the Islamist Menace

Elan Journo   January 16, 2016

Did you catch those breaking news reports, right after the San Bernardino shooting, suggesting that the attack was workplace violence? You might chalk that up to off-the-cuff speculation. Yet there was a kind of desperation behind the insistence on finding some generic, non-ideological motive. Yet it turned out to be what many expected from the outset, a jihadist attack; one of the murderers had pledged allegiance to Islamic State.

Think back to the mass shooting at Fort Hood in 2009. Officially, it was played down as workplace violence. Yet Nidal Hasan, a psychiatrist serving in the U.S. Army, viewed himself as a "soldier of Allah." When he gunned down thirteen people on the base, he shouted "Allahu Akbar."

Which brings us to the recent murderous ambush of a Philadelphia police officer, while he was sitting in his patrol car. The assailant shot at the officer at close range, inflicting serious injuries. Why?

"This was a criminal with a stolen gun" the mayor of Philadelphia insisted at a press conference. "In no way, shape or form does anybody in this room believe that Islam or the teaching of Islam" is connected with the attack. And yet:

> [I]mmediately after the mayor's pronouncement, the commander of the police department's homicide unit calmly took the microphone. Capt. James Clark reported that the shooter (later identified as 30-year-old Edward Archer) had said, repeatedly, that he followed Allah, that he pledged allegiance to Islamic State and "That is the reason I did what I did."

By now the pattern is familiar. We can see a determined reluctance, flowing into outright refusal, to acknowledge the Islamist menace. Reflecting on this phenomenon, Dorothy Rabinowitz of the *Wall Street Journal* lays the blame at the doorstep of the White House:

This blog post originally appeared in *The Times of Israel*.

> Years of effort by this administration to deny, conceal and
> sermonize the nation out of its awareness of facts clear-
> ly evident to them is the sort of thing that doesn't escape
> Americans in this election season, shadowed by the threat
> of terrorism.

Without question, the current administration has outdone itself
in dodging the issue. I talked about that a while back (see "War on
(Fill In the Misleading Blank)," page 73). But the problem is broader than Obama's policy, and it predates the current administration.

For years the smear of "Islamophobia" has worked to dampen serious discussion and critique of the Islamist movement. To find the
intellectuals and scholars and journalists vigorously shouting down
any such discussion, look to the left. Sam Harris has insightfully exposed the dishonesty of that smear, and the hypocrisy of leftist intellectuals who profess to uphold freedom and progress yet function as
apologists for barbarism.

Now, *even Michael Walzer*, an influential left-leaning political theo-
rist, is tired of this refusal to confront Islamists. Writing in *Dissent*, a
pillar of the left-wing intellectual establishment, Walzer admonishes
his brothers-in-arms. "I frequently come across leftists who are more
concerned with avoiding accusations of Islamophobia than they are
with condemning Islamist zealotry." Consequently, many are unable
to "consider the very good reasons for fearing Islamist zealots—and so
they have difficulty explaining what's going on in the world." It says a
lot about the gravity of the problem that Walzer was moved to write
this lengthy article. (I hesitate to recommend the article, because although it has some value, there's much to disagree with.)

At this point, you might form the impression that the refusal to
properly identify and define the Islamist movement (let alone criticize
it) is confined to leftist politicians and intellectuals. Not so.

George W. Bush took every opportunity to evade the nature of
Islamic totalitarianism. While the ruins of the World Trade Center
were still blazing, he gave speeches underscoring his belief that "the
terrorists have no home in any faith." On and on he went, hammering
at that theme, despite all the evidence to the contrary. For instance:
The 9/11 ringleader had written a note telling his team how to prepare
themselves: "Remember that this is a battle for the sake of God. As the
prophet, peace be upon him, said, 'An action for the sake of God is
better than all of what is in this world.' . . . Either end your life while
praying, seconds before the target, or make your last words: 'There is

no God but God, Muhammad is His messenger.'"

For at least the last fifteen years we have lived amid an intellectu-al smog—combining self-induced mental fog and the pollution of dis-honesty. One effect is to hinder our understanding of the character and aims of the Islamic totalitarian movement. Another effect is evi-dent in certain reactions to San Bernardino, Fort Hood, Philadelphia and other attacks. In these we can detect the workings of a kind of po-litical taboo, whose purpose is to discourage us from thinking about the Islamist movement at all.

For how much longer can we allow that taboo to go unchallenged?

Devaluing Secular Government?

Elan Journo January 23, 2016

The idea of separating religion from state was a major advance in political thought, yet massively undervalued. So much so that many in the West take it for granted. Two recent articles—one about Pakistan, another about France—underscore how that idea deserves greater appreciation and strengthening.

To grasp the importance of secular government, observe its negation in Pakistan. Consider the tragic story of one teenager, Anwar Ali. During a prayer meeting at the neighborhood mosque, he thought the imam asked who loves Muhammad, and naturally he raised his hand. But he had misheard the question; in fact the imam had asked who does not love the prophet. The imam denounced the boy for blasphemy, a crime punishable by death.

The story turns from awful to grisly. In shame the boy went home. He cut off his right hand. And he brought it back to the imam in penance. "What I did," the boy later said, "was for love of the Prophet Muhammad." His father said he felt lucky to have a son so devout. And doubtless the boy and his father really believe all that, but it is also a crucial factor that in allegations of blasphemy, as the *New York Times* reports, it is "nearly impossible for the accused to defend themselves in court. Even publicly repeating details of the accusation is tantamount to blasphemy in its own right."

That incident in Pakistan calls to mind life in Europe long ago, before the Age of Enlightenment, when the dominant religion of the time—then it was Christianity—denounced blasphemers and burned heretics. Politically, with the advent of secular government, we've come a long way since then.

But to grasp why the separation of religion from state must be bolstered within the West, consider an article in *The New Republic*.

Published a year after the attacks at *Charlie Hebdo*, the article pushes back on France's policy of secular government, known as "laicite." Broadly speaking, that policy encompasses freedom of religion, the separation of religion from government, and constraints on religious expression. Laicite was intended to block the influence of the Catholic

---

This blog post originally appeared in *The Times of Israel*.

church on affairs of state. And over all laicite is an admirable policy (though some applications, such as bans on religious attire, arguably infringe on individual freedom).

So, against the backdrop of the jihadist attacks at *Charlie Hebdo* and months later at multiple locations in Paris—attacks intended to punish France for failing to bow in submission; attacks carried out by holy warriors animated by the goal of a totalitarian Islamic society wherein religion and state are inseparable—*The New Republic* floats this outlandish suggestion, "Is it time for France to abandon Laicite?"

The article attempts to defend its proposal for rolling back laicite, but the argument conspicuously ignores the actual character and basic goal of the Islamic totalitarian movement, while harping on the at-best peripheral issue that some Muslims purportedly chafe at the country's secular laws. In the end the proposal boils down to appeasement of the Islamist movement.

It is revealing of our present intellectual climate that a reputable, intellectual magazine—for decades a bastion of American liberalism—has published an article that calls for putting hammer and chisel to the wall separating religion from state as a means of abating the threat from a cause seeking religious totalitarianism.

What's needed now more than ever is wider understanding and an uncompromising defense of the separation of religion from state as a cornerstone of a free society.

Fueling Iran's Hostility

Elan Journo   February 2, 2016

The Iran nuclear deal was the centerpiece of Obama's multi-year diplomatic campaign to extend a hand of friendship to Tehran. Six months later, where do things stand? Thanks to the deal, which includes lifting economic sanctions and paying out billions of dollars, Iran has reaped a financial windfall. Quite predictably, Iran has continued funding and arming jihadist groups. But another consequence of the deal—again, in line with predictions—deserves particular emphasis: Iran's swaggering disdain for us.

You can observe that in the words of the regime's president, Hassan Rouhani. While touring around Europe last month to recruit foreign investment, he explained that:

> The Americans know very well that when it comes to important regional issues [in the Middle East] they cannot achieve anything without Iran's influence or say. . . . It's possible that Iran and the United States might have friendly relations. But the key to that is in Washington's hands, not Tehran's.

Though hardly new, this Iranian presumption of holding the moral high ground is amped up. Our diplomatic wooing of the ayatollahs—and the nuclear deal in particular—has fueled it.

Beyond the financial reward, the deal bestowed on Iran an undeserved moral endorsement as a nation that can be dealt with through persuasion, despite its vicious character and goals. Whatever else our diplomats might say, mildly remonstrating with Iran here and there, we've given our affirmation that its theocratic regime is legitimate. A natural result of that was to increase the confidence of a regime that declares itself—and has proven to be—the vanguard of a holy war against the West. Moreover, you can see how our implied endorsement of Tehran would reinforce their view of America as morally bankrupt: economically and militarily, America is the world's most powerful nation, yet it stoops to appease a far weaker adversary. Thus we encourage in them contempt for us and (added) self-righteousness about

---

This blog post originally appeared in *The Times of Israel*.

their jihadist path.

The Iran deal has cast a searing light on an obscene spectacle. To adapt in the present context one of Ayn Rand's observations: America has assumed the role of a cringing, bargaining victim, while Iran stands as a self-righteous, resolute aggressor.

The Mythology of the Iran Nuclear Deal

Elan Journo   February 14, 2016

When defending the Iran nuclear deal, the Obama administration and its surrogates made claims that seemed, at least to some people, plausible. For a long time, I've argued that the deal was predicated on evading Iran's jihadist character and malignant goals, and that the deal's selling points were fantastical. Some people felt that "only time will tell"; so let's consider two of the administration's claims.

The nuclear deal, Barack Obama claimed, will "ensur[e] that all pathways to a bomb are cut off." This of course was a central pillar of the case for the deal. Remember the assurances about "anytime, anywhere" inspections of Iran's nuclear facilities? That was a hyped-up talking point that the administration quickly dropped. What about getting a full accounting of Iran's past nuclear research, including its military dimensions (such as warhead design)? No, according to John Kerry, we shouldn't be "fixated" on that, we just have to move on. What about the shutting of "all pathways" to a bomb? Listen to James Clapper, director of national intelligence, who testified before Congress this month: "We do not know whether Iran will eventually decide to build nuclear weapons," adding that if the regime "chooses to," it maintains the "ability to build missile-deliverable nuclear weapons."

Or consider another salient claim: by reintegrating Iran into the global economy, the deal could strengthen (putatively) friendly elements within Iran. Obama told one interviewer: "And then I think there are others inside Iran who think that [opposing the United States, seeking to destroy Israel, causing havoc in the region] is counterproductive. And it is possible that if we sign this nuclear deal, we strengthen the hand of those more moderate forces inside of Iran."

Predictably, the inflow of dollars has gone to Iran's state-owned or semistate-backed industries (the theocracy and its military vanguard dominate the economy). Reiterating what has been known for decades, James Clapper told Congress that the Tehran regime is "the foremost state sponsor of terrorism" and that Iran and its proxy forces "remain a continuing terrorist threat to U.S. interests and partners worldwide." Beyond the financial gains that bolster the regime, what impact has

---

This blog post originally appeared in *The Times of Israel*.

the deal had on Tehran's hostility toward us? It's fueled that hostility, as I argued in an earlier post, a fact that goes underappreciated.

Last week, with something like a "carnival atmosphere," tens of thousands marched in Tehran "chanting 'Death to America and Israel' and waving anti-Western placards," celebrating the "37th anniversary of the country's 1979 Islamic revolution." The regime actively inculcates animosity toward the West. Ponder the outlook of one 22-year-old Iranian who attended the festivities: "I am happy that I was able to come here today, and as an Iranian I can put my fist in America's mouth and say 'Death to America.'"

To revisit major selling points of the Iran nuclear deal is to see just how detached from reality they were.

The Misunderstood Mullahs

Elan Journo   March 31, 2016

A Review of *Iran's Deadly Ambition: The Islamic Republic's Quest for Global Power*, by Ilan Berman. New York: Encounter Books, 2015.

"No, Iran Isn't Destabilizing the Middle East." Paul Pillar's article in *The National Interest* a month before the Iran nuclear deal was signed attacked critics of the negotiations. Pillar disputed the "badly mistaken myth" that Tehran is "'destabilizing' the Middle East or seeking to 'dominate' it or exercise 'hegemony' over it, or that it is 'on the march' to take over the region." On the contrary, while we might dislike Iran's conduct—bolstering the Assad regime in Syria, backing Hezbollah in Lebanon, nourishing Hamas in Gaza, dominating what's left of Iraq, funding and training the Taliban in Afghanistan, and arming Islamist rebels in Yemen—Iran is simply reacting to its circumstances as any other state would. Iran's distinctive ideological character and stated goals, in other words, are at best peripheral to understanding and evaluating its conduct.

Pillar spent nearly thirty years as a senior intelligence analyst at the Central Intelligence Agency, and holds impeccable academic credentials. He can hardly be dismissed as a fringe figure. Indeed, the gist of his view—that we shouldn't worry about Iran's distinctive ideological character—informs the Obama administration's approach to Iran. The Obama team acknowledges Iran's pervasive violation of rights domestically, its wholesale backing of Islamist terrorism, and its ominous nuclear program. But these actions have little to do with one another, or with any larger strategic threat. Moreover, despite the weekly "Death to America" chants (merely "rhetorical excess," according to John Kerry) and the stated desire to wipe Israel off the map, Iran's leaders supposedly care chiefly about "regime survival" and the economic aspirations of their citizens—as if a brutal theocracy, deep down, wants what's best for its people. On the unstated premise that everyone in politics has a price, Obama has even suggested that the nuclear deal could entice Iran to improve its conduct while taking on its "rightful role" in the community of nations.

This article originally appeared in *The Claremont Review of Books*.

Ilan Berman, however, believes that the derivation of Iran's conduct from its ideology is missing from Washington policy discussions. In *Iran's Deadly Ambition*, Berman argues that the fundamental problem with Iran is not its nuclear quest, but the regime itself: Tehran is animated by "an uncompromising religious worldview that sees itself at war with the West."

> During the tumultuous decade of the 1980s, as [Ayatollah] Khomeini's revolutionaries consolidated power at home, the principle of "exporting the revolution" became a cardinal regime priority. Its importance was demonstrated in the fact that, despite the expense of a bloody, grinding eight-year war with Saddam Hussein's Iraq, the fledgling Islamic Republic sunk colossal resources into becoming a hub of "global resistance."

Three decades later, Tehran remains committed to this vision. Even as we negotiate with Iran over its nuclear program, its leaders are "busy translating their vision of world influence into action."

Berman offers a measured, data-rich survey of Iran's jihadist ambition, an ambition encompassing far more than the nuclear program. The jihadist group Lebanese Hezbollah (literally, "army of Allah") was founded with Tehran's support in the mid 1980s to implement Khomeini's political theory of clerical rule. Hezbollah has become Iran's main proxy force in Syria. Iraq, Europe and Africa. Citing reports compiled by the State Department, Berman shows that Iranian sponsorship of global terrorism continues unabated.

In Iraq, Tehran backed insurgents that undermined and killed American forces. Over time, the new Baghdad government fell under Tehran's dominion. In Afghanistan, Iran lavished millions of dollars to buy the loyalty of government officials: five years ago, Hamid Karzai, the president of Afghanistan at the time, admitted to accepting a $2 million payoff from Tehran. And lately, Iran has bolstered the resurgent Taliban with shipments of arms, ammunition, rocket-propelled grenades, mortars and plastic explosives. In Syria, Iran continued to back the Assad regime, even while Tehran was subject to severe economic sanctions.

Iran advances its agenda, Berman shows, through international enablers, notably China and North Korea. From Pyongyang, which now possesses nuclear weapons, Iran received technological know-how and help procuring materials for its own nuclear program. Beijing relies heavily on Iranian natural gas and petroleum, a trade relationship that has yielded diplomatic benefits for Tehran. China, along with Russia, frequently blocked the imposition of U.N. sanctions on Iran's nuclear program. To circumvent economic sanctions, Iran has found willing allies in Latin America, where its diplomatic footprint has grown. Venezuela, for instance, abetted Tehran in channeling foreign currency through an Iranian-owned local bank.

Berman describes the complex, wide-ranging web of political schemes, diplomatic stratagems, and lethal campaigns, military and terrorist, radiating from Tehran. Examine that web, work through the implications, and it becomes clear that Iran is defined by its ideological vision. Yet, as Berman notes, Washington ignores Tehran's character, resulting in an Iran policy predicated more on "aspiration than reality."

Iran's Deadly Ambition provides a superb, albeit alarming portrait of the Iranian regime. It is alarming, not merely because of the scale of Iran's militant ambition, but also because the prevailing American assessment of the regime is so disconnected from abundant, plainly evident facts. By fixing our attention on Iran's ideological character, this book can help anchor U.S. policy in aspirations that accept rather than deny reality

What Unites the Jihadists

Elan Journo April 21, 2016

March 22: suicide bombings at Brussels airport and on the city's metro. March 27: a suicide bombing at a crowded park in Lahore, Pakistan. The differences between these attacks are considerable, and a mainstream perspective would have us focus on that data narrowly. But to understand these attacks—and to assess the jihadist menace—we need to give serious attention to their underlying commonality.

Look at the particulars in each case, and you find umpteen points of difference. Behind each attack, a different group. The Islamic State mounted the Brussels attack; the Pakistani Taliban deployed one of its fighters to the park in Lahore. The capabilities of these groups differ. Clearly ISIS has a reach surpassing the Pakistani Taliban. To this you can add the fact that jihadist groups engage in ferocious infighting. Many factions have different state sponsors that despise each other. The more you dig into these groups, the more dissimilar, the more disconnected, they can appear.

But such a concrete-bound perspective subverts our understanding. It opens the way for pseudo-explanations that have hampered our ability to combat this menace. George W. Bush relied on evasive definitions that whipsawed from the nebulous ("terrorists," "evil doers") to the ultra-narrow (it's al-Qaeda!). The Obama administration reprised the generic label "terrorists" and then emphasized "al-Qaeda" until the rise of ISIS (supposedly the JV team) made that risible; now we're supposed to combat "violent extremism," born of economic privation and lack of political voice.

What this betrays is much more than linguistic confusion. It reveals an underlying conceptual failure: the failure properly to understand and define the nature of the enemy. That's a necessary condition for combatting it effectively, a point confirmed by the policy failures of Bush and of Obama.

Instead we need to recognize what's distinctive—and so dangerous—about the jihadists. No, it's not primarily their use of terrorist means; nor any political or economic hardships. What unites them is their ideological goal. Despite their differences, they do in fact

---

This article originally appeared in *The Federalist*.

constitute an ideological movement—a movement long inspired and funded by patrons such as Iran, Saudi Arabia and the Gulf states.

Fundamentally, the diverse jihadist factions are united by a common end. They fight to create a society subjugated to religious law (sharia), wherever they can. They seek Islamic totalitarianism. Hearing that, some people balk: Can we really put in one category the Pakistani Taliban, the Afghan Taliban, Islamic State, al-Qaeda, Hezbollah, Hamas, Boko Haram, the Muslim Brotherhood, the Iranian regime, and many others—despite their sectarian, ethnic, regional and language differences?

Yes, because what they strive for is essentially the same. How they seek to realize that goal—strategically and tactically—certainly differs: outright war; terrorism; indoctrination and ballot boxes; some combination of these. But these varied means are geared to the same ultimate end.

And of course they fight against one another, for dominance, for turf, for doctrinal reasons (recall how al-Qaeda disowned ISIS). Such infighting is a feature of ideological movements. For example, there are many varieties of socialists. The British Fabians emphasized education; Lenin was committed to revolution. And there were notorious intra-movement fights: for example, Stalin sent a hit squad to liquidate one rival, Leon Trotsky. The Soviets in Moscow were at odds with the communist rulers in China. The broad common aim, however, was to rid the world of capitalism in the name of imposing state control of the means of production.

With the jihadists, their common theocratic aim is reflected in how they identify their enemies. Their doctrine holds that the path to political supremacy entails a return to piety and the imposition of the "Truth" far and wide, putting to death whoever stands in the way. An enemy is anyone who fails to submit to their religious dogma, including (but not limited to) apostates, heretics (e.g., Muslims of the wrong sect), atheists and assorted unbelievers. For the Muslim Brotherhood in Egypt, a progenitor of the Islamic totalitarian movement, a major focus was on Arab regimes deemed impious. The Islamic State—like al-Qaeda, like the Iranian regime—puts emphasis on the West, with its secular society, man-made laws, and infidel population.

The Lahore bombing underlines just how wrong the prevailing view of the jihadists really is. It's common today to hear how jihadists are moved primarily by economic and political grievances. That would mean that those families lining up for the bumper cars at the fairground in Lahore were slaughtered because they had somehow thwarted the Pakistani Taliban from getting decent jobs and the vote. But in reality the Taliban has it in for Pakistan's Christian minority (who are deemed unbelievers). Many people in the thronged park that day were Christians celebrating Easter.

Moreover, we've heard a great deal about the (relative) poverty of the Molenbeek neighborhood in Brussels, and how some of the "martyrs" who carried out the Paris attacks last November had been petty criminals. Relevant, perhaps; causally fundamental, no. In a "martyrdom video" that ISIS released in January, what do the Paris jihadists themselves tell us? They're at war with us because we're "unbelievers"; they're angry that we oppose the Islamic State in its quest to entrench a totalitarian Islamic society.

Over the last fifteen years, we've witnessed two U.S. administrations evade the responsibility of understanding the Islamic totalitarian movement. And we've witnessed those two administrations fail to defeat it. If we are to succeed at that goal, a crucial first step is to understand the enemy we face. We need to grasp that while Islamic totalitarianism is a multiform movement, it is fundamentally united by its religious doctrine and vicious goal. Only then can we fully understand Brussels and Lahore and Paris and Ankara and San Bernardino and Beirut, and the long, bloody trail of jihad. Only then can we grasp the scope of the Islamist menace and effectively combat it, bringing into focus the need to confront the states that inspire and sponsor it.

After Orlando: Why Trump and Clinton Both Get the Jihadists Wrong

Elan Journo June 15, 2016

What we do know so far about the mass shooting in Orlando: in a 911 call, the killer at the Pulse nightclub pledged allegiance to Islamic State, and he had previously expressed a fervent desire to become a "martyr." In their speeches responding to the massacre, Hillary Clinton and Donald Trump each sought to demonstrate a firmer, clearer grasp of the jihadist menace—and therefore prove themselves best positioned to combat it. Each channeled one of the prevalent views in our culture. Both, however, are profoundly wrong. Both are united, ironically enough, in negating the crucial role of ideas in animating the jihadist cause.

The view Trump put forward, which appeals to many people, is meant to sound like a serious, factual account. "We are importing Radical Islamic Terrorism into the West through a failed immigration system." Because Trump has frequently mouthed the words "radical Islam," some people believe this view constitutes plain-speaking. But instead of conceptualizing the enemy as an ideological movement—one that people join because they choose to embrace particular ideas and doctrines—the account Trump has voiced negates the role of ideas. Essentially, it is a tribalist outlook, dividing the world into us vs. them—America vs. the outsiders

But it turns out that the killer in Orlando was born—like Trump himself—in New York. Revealingly, the blame is put on the fact that the killer's parents were Afghan immigrants: "The bottom line is that the only reason the killer was in America in the first place was because we allowed his family to come here." That applies equally to generations of Americans, the vast majority of whom were law abiding citizens. So for Trump, the blame falls on the killer's outsider bloodline. His parents came from a faraway land, so he is forever an outsider; his beliefs and chosen actions are irrelevant. On this view, the tag "radical Islam" turns out to be vacuous: far from designating a substantive conception of the jihadist cause, in fact it serves as a shorthand for tribalist bigotry against outsiders (which manifests as outright racism

---

This blog post originally appeared in *The Times of Israel*.

when Trump applies it to Hispanics).

You can see that in the depressingly popular "solution" of enacting a sweeping ban on Muslim immigration. Obviously, a rational immigration policy must bar entry to individuals seeking to violate our rights (thus barring anyone with ties to or membership in Islamist groups and organizations), while allowing entry to individuals seeking to live and work peacefully. The proposed ban, however, starts with the opposite, tribalist premise. Outsiders: bad. Maybe some will turn out to be OK, but don't count on it.

Notice how this view wipes out a crucial distinction, one that's necessary for understanding the jihadist cause. While all jihadists are followers of Islam, it is blatantly false that all Muslims are jihadists. It should go without saying, though today it is necessary to say so, that countless Muslims are law-abiding, peaceful, productive Americans. Jihadists, by contrast, are individuals who choose to join an ideological cause, a cause intent on the totalitarian imposition of Islamic religious law. What distinguishes the jihadists is not any inborn tribal identity, but the vicious political-ideological vision they strive to realize. It is this ideological factor that the tribalist view negates.

So does the marginally more sophisticated perspective that Hillary Clinton conveyed in her post-Orlando speech. The killer, she insisted, was a *"madman* filled with hate, . . . [a] horrible sense of vengeance and vindictiveness in his heart, . . . rage." [Emphasis added] Here, emotion and above all, some form of madness are taken as fundamental. Therefore, we're instructed, more has to be done to address the persistent *"virus that poisoned his mind."* [Emphasis added.]

Where, then, does his 911 call, swearing fidelity to the caliphate, fit in to this causal narrative? Or his stated wish to become a martyr? Or the reports of him bellowing "Allahu Akbar" as he sprayed bullets into the crowd? These data points reflect a certain ideological outlook. That's precisely what Clinton's view trivializes. And in doing so, it forecloses anything that might resemble a sensible policy for combatting the threat.

The same is true of a variation of the Clintonian narrative, which puts even greater emphasis on mental illness. People who are mentally ill, writes Jeet Heer in *The New Republic*, can be drawn to an "extremist ideology," so, a "mental-health framework has to be a key part of the solution no less than other policy initiatives"—at least on par with everything else. We can agree that many factors are at play in explaining the actions of a given individual. But it is a serious mistake to downgrade ideology as just one factor among many, precisely because of its immense power over people's minds, a fact evident in umpteen jihadist attacks. (Besides, you can make a strong claim that espousing jihadist doctrine is a kind of detachment from reality: for example, what else can it mean to seek "martyrdom"?)

These prevailing views get the jihadists wrong. We need to grasp that fundamentally the jihadists are moved by the ideas they accept and choose to act on. To view this from a wider perspective, note that the communists were moved by their ideal of "from each according to his ability, to each according to his need," erecting dictatorial regimes to put their vision into practice. And that cause attracted some of the worst specimens of humanity, power-lusting thugs, haters of achievement, and psychotics among them. Note that the Founding Fathers, by contrast, upheld the ideals of individualism and reason as the foundation of a free society, creating a constitutional republic to safeguard individual rights. And their cause appealed strongly to productive, independent people seeking a better life. The larger point is that philosophic ideas—whether true or false—are crucial in human life and in understanding cultural-political movements.

That point is lost to many people today, especially the leading presidential candidates. They fail to understand the centrality of philosophic ideas in animating the jihadist cause. The last two administrations failed properly to define the nature of the Islamist movement. Look around—we're living with the consequences of their irrational policies. Fitting within that dismal tradition, Clinton and Trump have put forward views that negate the ideological character of the enemy, and so neither has the understanding necessary to deal effectively with the mounting threat we face.

PART 5

The Distinctiveness of an Objectivist Approach to Foreign Policy

Paul Ryan, Ayn Rand, and U.S. Foreign Policy

Elan Journo October 2012

Vice-presidential candidate Paul Ryan has credited philosopher Ayn Rand with inspiring him to enter politics—and made her 1,000-plus-page magnum opus, *Atlas Shrugged*, required reading for his staff. "The reason I got involved in public service, by and large, if I had to credit one thinker, one person, it would be Ayn Rand," he said in 2005 at a gathering of Rand fans. "The fight we are in here, make no mistake about it, is a fight of individualism versus collectivism." It is a theme that pervades Rand's corpus.[1] While Ryan has distanced himself from Rand's philosophy of Objectivism, he continues to express admiration for *Atlas Shrugged*.

The addition of the Wisconsin congressman to the GOP ticket naturally unleashed a flash-mob of analysts parsing his speeches, articles and signature proposals for evidence of her influence. On domestic policy, the impact[2] of Rand's ideas[3] on Ryan's outlook[4] is marked, though uneven and sometimes overstated. Religion, in particular, has driven a wedge between Ryan, who would enact Catholic dogma into law,[5] and Rand, an atheist, who championed the separation of church and state. But what has received far less attention is Ryan's outlook on foreign policy—and whether it bears the mark of Rand's thought.

Ayn Rand's foreign policy, if we can construct one from her writings, would be grounded in her view of man's rights and the nature of government.[6] Like the Founding Fathers, Rand argues that the ideal government is the servant, not the master, of the individual. In her view, it is a vital institution strictly limited to one function: to safeguard individual rights. By "rights," Rand means freedom to take "all the actions required by the nature of a rational being for the support, the furtherance, the fulfillment and the enjoyment of his own life." Critically, the protection of an individual's rights "does not mean that others must provide him with the necessities of life."[7]

Domestically, this outlook entails a truly free market with absolute legal protection of private property, and without regulations, bailouts, corporate handouts or entitlement programs like Social Security, Medicaid and Medicare. (Ryan breaks with Rand by attempting to

---

An earlier version of this article appeared in *Foreign Policy* on August 28, 2012.

save, rather than end these programs.) In Rand's political philosophy, however, there is no gulf between economic rights and personal and intellectual ones: for instance, she wrote passionately of the crucial importance (contra Ryan) of the right to abortion,[9] and regarded freedom of speech[10] as sacrosanct.

Like her views on domestic policy, a Randian foreign policy would be guided exclusively by the goal of protecting the individual rights of Americans, and only Americans. Accordingly, the U.S. government shouldn't issue handouts to other countries (through foreign aid or international welfare schemes), nor treat its citizens as cannon fodder (through a military draft). Indeed, Rand was scathing in her analyses of the Vietnam War, arguing that it did not serve America's national interest. "[I]t is a pure instance of blind, senseless altruistic self-sacrificial slaughter," she wrote in *Capitalism: The Unknown Ideal*.[11]

Of course, there are times when government is obligated to go to war, according to Rand. The crucial standard here is whether the lives and property of Americans are imperiled. The only morally justifiable purpose for war, she wrote, is self-defense. This rules out so-called humanitarian missions, like the tragic 1992–93 mission in Somalia, and the notion that the United States is somehow obliged to serve as the world's policeman. The primary function of the military, in Rand's eyes, should be to deter and, when necessary, defeat foreign aggressors.

Rand regarded any form of pacifism[12] (including Ron Paul-esque passivity) as destructive to national defense. And undoubtedly she would have supported a strong military response to the 9/11 attacks (though, as I have argued in my book,[13] and sketch out below, she would have rejected George W. Bush's conception of the enemy and his entire prosecution of the war).

Rand viewed deterrence as an especially important—and effective—method of defending American freedom. In her view, the power of a morally confident, assertive United States was considerable, though largely unappreciated. For instance, she believed that if the West had truly stood up to the Soviet bloc by withdrawing its moral sanction, ending the flow of aid, and imposing an airtight boycott, the Soviet threat would have disintegrated many years before it actually did, without the need for war.

Perhaps most importantly, Rand argued in favor of genuine free trade—without trade barriers, protective tariffs or special privileges. In her words: "the opening of the world's trade routes to free international trade and competition among the private citizens of all countries dealing directly with one another." In the nineteenth century, she argued, free trade liberated the world by "undercutting and wrecking the remnants of feudalism and the statist tyranny of absolute monarchies." Not coincidentally, she observed, this era enjoyed the longest period of general peace in human history (roughly from 1815 to 1914).[14]

Taken together, Rand's approach entails a foreign policy based on the morality of "rational self-interest." To illustrate what that would look like, let us bring Rand's approach to bear on several of today's major foreign policy issues, starting with Iran.

Tehran is a leader of the Islamist movement, the cause animating al-Qaeda, the Taliban, the Muslim Brotherhood and kindred groups. Iran has inspired and funded jihadist terrorism and cast itself as an embodiment of the movement's political ideal. It's a regime that tramples on the rights of its own citizens. It ambitiously seeks to kill and subjugate beyond its borders, and, owing to its jihadist ideology, is vociferously anti-American. From Washington's capitulation in the hostage crisis of 1979–80, the regime concluded that it could get away with committing an act of war against America. Rand noted at the time that because we failed to march in with force within days after the hostage taking, the repercussions would be severe.

Since then U.S. policymakers, in effect, rewarded Iran's aggression with bribes and conciliation, and thereby encouraged a spiral of further Iranian-backed attacks.[15] Witness the Hezbollah hijacking of a TWA airliner; the kidnapping and torture of Americans in Lebanon; the 1983 bombings of the U.S. Embassy in Beirut and, later, the barracks of U.S. Marines, killing 241 Americans. The 9/11 Commission linked[16] Tehran to at least eight of the suicide hijackers. Later, Iranian forces trained and armed Iraqi and Afghan insurgents,[17] who murdered U.S. troops. Considering the U.S. failure to recognize the Iranian regime's character and goals, and assertively end its aggression, Tehran's defiance over its nuclear program should hardly surprise.

We are at war with Iran, but only that country knows it; in the name of self-defense, the U.S. government is morally obliged to eliminate this enemy. A military option is a non-starter, however, in the shadow of the Iraq and Afghanistan failures (more on those in a moment). But even when we have the opportunity to morally support the Iranian people in attempting to remove from power a regime hostile to the freedom of Americans and Iranians alike, as we did with the Green Movement, which arose after the 2009 elections, we refuse to do so. The reputedly crippling sanctions now in place are of course a forlorn hope, especially considering the large-enough-to-drive-a-truck-through exemptions[18] that have already been granted.

Part of what has magnified the tragedy of 9/11 is the failure of policymakers to properly identify and vigorously pursue the enemy that attacked us. It was not simply the hijackers' al-Qaeda cell, but the jihadist movement, spearheaded by Tehran and bankrolled by Saudi wealth, which had been waging attacks against us for years. In my book, *Winning the Unwinnable War,*[19] I discuss the nature and malignant goal of that movement, and explore what went wrong in the U.S. response, particularly the policy fiascos in Iraq and Afghanistan.

The goal uniting these two wars was Bush's messianic policy of "nation building" and bringing the vote to the oppressed and needy of the Middle East. Clearing out sewage pipes, fixing up hospitals, printing textbooks—these welfare and social services projects may be the province of the Peace Corps, but not the Army Corps, nor is it right to risk the lives of American soldiers for the sake of the world's needy. Just as Rand decried Vietnam as a selfless, purposeless war, so that same criticism applies, as strongly, in Iraq. Much of what went wrong in Iraq and Afghanistan stemmed from a policy of putting an altruistic welfare agenda first, above the self-interested goal of eliminating whatever threat we faced in those countries.

Tragically, despite its unparalleled military strength, the United States mired itself, needlessly, in no-win wars. Baghdad is now under Tehran's sway.[20] The continuing strife in Iraq, marked by only occasional suicide bombings,[21] is a testament to how the notion of success has been progressively defined down. In Afghanistan there are no longer good options. A minimum step toward the right policy—one with a modicum of justice to the now 2,000 American who perished there—is to properly redefine the mission from perpetual "nation building" to expunging the Taliban and allied Islamist forces in Afghanistan and the Pakistani borderlands.

One recent bright spot, seemingly, was the Arab Spring. But the upheavals across the Middle East, it turned out, shared only superficial similarities. One trend that did emerge, though, was the ascendance, notably in Egypt and Tunisia, of political parties sympathetic to or fully embracing Islamist goals. Here, then, is the consummation of Bush's "nation-building" democracy crusade. We now must contend with the emerging threat of an Egypt dominated by Islamists—a regime that our diplomats have been falling over themselves to encourage. At minimum we should refuse to endorse the regime (even though popularly elected) and even shun it.[22] To embrace it is to lend the regime an unde-served legitimacy; if any genuinely freedom-seeking Egyptians remain, would they feel anything but demoralized at the spectacle?[23]

U.S. policy has galvanized one group: Islamists. Further evidence of that came on September 11, 2012, in the form of the conspicuously timed attacks on our embassies in Cairo and Benghazi.

Storming the sovereign territory of the world's militarily stron-gest nation requires considerable temerity. Islamists in Egypt, howev-er, thought nothing of attempting to invade the mission in Cairo and hoisting their flag. In Libya, in what looks like a meticulously calcu-lated assault, the self-professed soldiers of Allah managed to murder the U.S. ambassador and three other Americans. The uproar and ri-ots across the region, putatively in reaction to a YouTube video crit-ical of Islam, brought to the surface (yet again) the assertiveness of those who seek obedience to religious dogma and revile the free mind and the individual's freedom of speech. What inspires not fear but contempt in the hearts of our Islamist enemies is the meekness of American foreign policy across decades.[24]

Meshing with that broad pattern, the Obama administration's response to the embassy crisis was deplorable. It's hard to imagine a more self-abasing reaction than to have the Cairo embassy apologize to the raging mob, while disparaging free speech. Nor can anyone take our government's commitment to freedom of speech seriously when it tries to lean on YouTube to take down the video, and rather than com-mitting to protect the safety of the man behind the film, gives him a perp walk. Compared with that, the Romney-Ryan response was bet-ter: Yes, America has projected weakness; yes, Washington has under-cut real allies, for example, by seeking to distance itself from Israel.

But that's far short of what was necessary. At minimum, our lead-ers should declare that American lives are untouchable and that our freedom of speech is inviolable, and demonstrate a willingness, in ac-tion, to retaliate with force. (When questioned about the embassy cri-sis in the vice-presidential debate, Ryan was handed an opportunity to speak forcefully in defense of freedom of speech and the sanctity of the rights of Americans. He dodged it.)

Consider, finally, our defense budget.[25] Clouding the debate over de-fense spending is the fact that our present foreign policy leads us to en-gage in a mess of contradictions: legitimate, self-defensive operations; ille-gitimate humanitarian, "nation building" efforts (along with all the sup-port costs for long-term bases); and the occasional disbursal of bribes[26] to our enemies. First, strip out the global-welfare category. Next, consider whether we would need every single one of our permanent overseas bases—if our foreign policy demonstrated in word and deed our willingness, when necessary, to crush enemies. Arguably, we could make do with fewer—and realize considerable savings. To safeguard the freedom of Americans, a powerful, well-equipped and technologically advanced military—one that is peerless, efficient and formidable—is essential. Yet there's reason to think, under a principled, self-interested approach, we'd have the strong military we need, at a lesser cost.

What's distinctive to an approach informed by Rand's ideas is that it hinges on a rethinking of the moral values that should inform foreign policy. At its core is the idea that the individual[27] has a right to his life, that he's morally entitled to live it in line with his rational judgment,[28] and that his freedom to act on his judgment must be safeguarded from aggressors. And, crucially, he bears no duty selflessly to serve others— whether they are next door or overseas. This animating premise enjoins a firm, long-range policy of assertive national defense and strictly rules out altruistic[29] missions à la Bush.

Clearly, Paul Ryan does not share Rand's foreign policy. But is there nevertheless a discernible influence?

Reading Ryan's most substantive speech[30] on foreign policy, delivered at the Hamilton Society in 2011, you can certainly hear the reverberation of Ayn Rand's ideas. "[I]f you believe these rights are universal human rights, then that clearly forms the basis of your views on foreign policy," he said, partially echoing the Randian conviction that regimes are moral to the degree that they respect individual rights. For Ryan, as for Rand, championing rights leads "you to reject moral relativism. It causes you to recoil at the idea of persistent moral indifference toward any nation that stifles and denies liberty." Though as already noted, Ryan did not speak forcefully in defense of free speech in the aftermath of the Libyan attacks. But at least there is, in line with Rand, a thoughtful promotion of free trade. In his Hamilton Society speech, for instance, he argued in favor of an "expanding community of nations that shares our economic values as well as our political values" in order to "ensure a more prosperous world."

If these similarities between the two are meaningful, Ryan nevertheless seems to fundamentally part ways with Rand. In particular, he speaks of the need to "renew our commitment to the idea that America is the greatest force for human freedom the world has ever seen," and sees in the Arab Spring the "long-repressed populations give voice to the fundamental desire for liberty." (The ethnic-sectarian bloodbath that ensued in Iraq was proof, if any were needed, that political freedom and peace are not an innate yearning of mankind.[31]) Further, Ryan claims that it is "always in the interest of the United States to promote these principles in other nations." Like President George W. Bush, whose wars he supported, Ryan appears to subscribe to the quasi-religious view that freedom is written into the soul of mankind, and that it is somehow the moral duty of America, the freest and wealthiest of nations, to go forth and wage wars to unchain the world's oppressed. In all this, he could not be less aligned with Rand.

Rand certainly believed that the United States benefits from a freer world. Thus, she held, America should speak up for dissidents everywhere who seek greater freedom. But Rand would only ever consider deploying the military where the rights of Americans hang in the balance—when, in other words, it becomes an issue of self-defense. This critical distinction may well be lost on Ryan, if the media's parsing of his neoconservative leanings has been fair.

Perhaps, in these waning days of the campaign season, Ryan will consider rereading Rand's work, and sharing it with his running mate. Anyone seeking to inject more rational and more distinctively American ideas into our nation's chaotic foreign policy ought to seriously consider Ayn Rand's refreshingly clear-eyed perspective.

Endnotes

1. The quote from Ryan appears in Ryan Lizza, "How Paul Ryan Captured the G.O.P.," *New Yorker*, 6 August 2012, http://www.newyorker.com/ reporting/2012/08/06/120806fa_fact_lizza#ixzz24lX7Q8jX (accessed 25 September 2012).

2. Don Watkins, "Ryan, Rand, and Rights," *Daily Caller*, 17 August 2012, http:// dailycaller.com/2012/08/17/ryan-rand-and-rights/ (accessed 25 September 2012).

3. Onkar Ghate, "Ayn Rand's Appeal," Fox News, 21 August 2012, http://www .foxnews.com/opinion/2012/08/21/ayn-rand-appeal/ (accessed 25 September 2012).

4. Don Watkins, "Why Paul Ryan Is No Ayn Rand on Social Security," *Christian Science Monitor*, 21 August 2012, http://www.csmonitor.com/Commentary/ Opinion/2012/0821/Why-Paul-Ryan-is-no-Ayn-Rand-on-Social-Security (accessed 25 September 2012).

5. Michelle Goldberg, "Paul Ryan's Extreme Abortion Views," *Daily Beast*, 11 August 2012, http://www.thedailybeast.com/articles/2012/08/11/paul-ryan-s-extreme-abortion-views.html (accessed 25 September 2012).http://www.thedailybeast. com/articles/2012/08/11/paul-ryan-s-extreme-abortion-views.html

6. Ayn Rand, "The Nature of Government," *The Virtue of Selfishness* (New York: Signet, 1964), http://www.aynrand.org/site/PageServer?pagename=arc_ayn_ rand_the_nature_of_government.

7. Ayn Rand, "Man's Rights," *Capitalism: the Unknown Ideal* (New York: Signet, 1986), http://www.aynrand.org/site/PageServer?pagename=arc_ayn_rand_man_ rights.

8. "Capitalism," *The Ayn Rand Lexicon*, http://aynrandlexicon.com/lexicon/ capitalism.html.

9. "Abortion," *The Ayn Rand Lexicon*, http://aynrandlexicon.com/lexicon/abortion.html.

10. "Free Speech," *The Ayn Rand Lexicon* http://aynrandlexicon.com/lexicon/free_ speech.html.

11. Ayn Rand, *Capitalism: The Unknown Ideal* (New York, NY: Signet, 1967), p. 224.

12. "Pacifism," *The Ayn Rand Lexicon*, http://aynrandlexicon.com/lexicon/pacifism.html.

13. Elan Journo, *Winning the Unwinnable War: America's Self-Crippled Response to Islamic Totalitarianism* (Lanham, MD: Lexington Books, 2009), http://www.amazon .com/dp/B003UERGVY.

14. "Foreign Policy," *The Ayn Rand Lexicon*, http://aynrandlexicon.com/lexicon/ foreign_policy.html#order_2.

15. Thomas Joscelyn, *Iran's Proxy War Against America*, The Claremont Institute, 2007, https://www.claremont.org/repository/docLib/20071127_ ProxyWarAgainstAmerica.pdf.

16. Daniel Pipes, "Iran's Link to Al-Qaeda: The 9/11 Commission's Evidence," *Middle East Forum*, Fall 2004, http://www.meforum.org/670/irans-link-to-al-qaeda-the-9-11-commissions (accessed 25 September 2012).

17. Michael R. Gordon and Andrew W. Lehren, "Leaked Reports Detail Iran's Aid for Iraqi Militias," *New York Times*, 22 October 2010 http://www.nytimes.com/2010/10/23/world/middleeast/23iran.html (accessed 28 September 2012); Sanjeev Miglani, " General McChrystal Says Afghan Insurgents Trained in Iran," Reuters, 30 May 2010, http://www.reuters.com/article/2010/05/30/us-afghanistan-iran-idUSTRE64T0U920100530 (accessed 28 September 2012).

18. David Feith, "Obama's Iran Loopholes," *Wall Street Journal*, 2 July 2012, http://online.wsj.com/article/SB10001424052702304211804577502912009234948.html (accessed 25 September 2012).

19. See: http://winningtheunwinnablewar.com/.

20. Josh Rogin, "US Struggles with Iran for Influence in Iraq," *Foreign Policy*, 23 March 2012, http://thecable.foreignpolicy.com/posts/2012/03/23/us_struggles_with_iran_for_influence_in_iraq (accessed 25 September 2012).

21. Yasir Ghazi, "Wave of Attacks Kill Dozens in Iraq," *New York Times*, 16 August 2012, http://www.nytimes.com/2012/08/17/world/middleeast/at-least-39-killed-in-wave-of-attacks-in-iraq.html?_r=1 (accessed 25 September 2012).

22. Christopher Bartolotta and Jordan McGillis, "A Conversation with Yaron Brook and Elan Journo," *Whitehead Journal of Diplomacy*, Winter/Spring 2012, http://blogs.shu.edu/diplomacy/2012/04/a-conversation-with-yaron-brook-and-elan-journo/ (accessed 25 September 2012).

23. Nick Meo, "US Secretary of State Hillary Clinton Meets Egypt's Muslim Brotherhood President Mohammed Morsi in Historic First," *Telegraph*, 14 July 2012, http://www.telegraph.co.uk/news/worldnews/africaandindianocean/egypt/9400749/US-Secretary-of-State-Hillary-Clinton-meets-Egypts-Muslim-Brotherhood-president-Mohammed-Morsi-in-historic-first.html (accessed 25 September 2012).

24. Elan Journo, "Our Self-Crippled Foreign Policy Encouraged Deadly Embassy Attack," FoxNews.com, 28 September 2012, http://www.foxnews.com/opinion/2012/09/28/our-self-crippled-policy-encouraged-deadly-embassy-attacks/ (accessed 28 September 2012).

25. http://www.economist.com/blogs/democracyinamerica/2011/12/defence-spending

26. Amit R. Paley, "Iraqis Joining Insurgency Less for Cause than Cash," *Washington Post*, 20 November 2007, http://www.washingtonpost.com/wp-dyn/content/article/2007/11/19/AR2007111902022.html (accessed 25 September 2012).

27. "Individualism," *The Ayn Rand Lexicon*, http://aynrandlexicon.com/lexicon/individualism.html.

28. "Independence," *The Ayn Rand Lexicon*, http://aynrandlexicon.com/lexicon/independence.html.

29. "Altruism," *The Ayn Rand Lexicon*, http://aynrandlexicon.com/lexicon/altruism.html.

30. House of Representatives Committee on the Budget, http://budget.house.gov/news/documentsingle.aspx?DocumentID=244386.

31. Richard A. Oppel Jr., "Number of Unidentified Bodies Found in Baghdad Rose Sharply in May," *New York Times*, 2 June 2007, http://www.nytimes.com/2007/06/02/world/middleeast/02iraq.html (accessed 25 September 2012).

Winning the Unwinnable War: America's Self-Crippled Response to Islamic Totalitarianism

Lexington Books, 2009

Edited by Elan Journo

Winning the Unwinnable War shows how our own policy ideas led to 9/11 and then crippled our response in the Middle East, and it makes the case for an unsettling conclusion: by subordinating military victory to perverse, allegedly moral constraints, Washington's policy has undermined our national security. Owing to the significant influence of Just War Theory and neoconservatism, the Bush administration consciously put the imperative of shielding civilians and bringing them elections above the goal of eliminating real threats to our security. Consequently, this policy left our enemies stronger, and America weaker, than before. The dominant alternative to Bush-esque idealism in foreign policy—so-called realism—has made a strong comeback under the tenure of Barack Obama. But this non-judgmental, supposedly practical, approach is precisely what helped unleash the enemy prior to 9/11.

The message of the essays in this thematic collection is that only by radically rethinking our foreign policy in the Middle East can we achieve victory over the enemy that attacked us on 9/11. We need a new moral foundation for our Mideast policy. That new starting point for U.S. policy is the moral ideal championed by the philosopher Ayn Rand: rational self-interest. Implementing this approach entails objectively defining our national interest as protecting the lives and freedoms of Americans—and then taking principled action to safeguard them. The book lays out the necessary steps for achieving victory and for securing America's long-range interests in the volatile Middle East.

"Fighting for victory may sound obvious but Journo, Epstein, and Brook show how remote the goal of victory is from current U.S. policy in the Middle East, which they characterize as based on 'a welfare mission to serve the poor and oppressed.' Instead of this unwinnable approach, the authors offer a robust and unapologetic re-assertion of American national interests, and they do so with a bracing eloquence that left this reader elated."

—Daniel Pipes, director of the *Middle East Forum*

TABLE OF CONTENTS

Read the Introduction and two sample chapters online:

AynRand.org/war-book

Buy the Kindle or paperback edition: https://amzn.com/0739135414

What You Can Do

To explore the ideas presented in this book further, visit
AynRand.org/Failing.

Read

"Man's Rights" by Ayn Rand

"If one wishes to advocate a free society," writes Ayn Rand, "one must realize that its indispensable foundation is the principle of individual rights." This essay defines and explains the principle of individual rights.

"Nature of Government" by Ayn Rand

This is a presentation of the Objectivist view of the nature and proper role of government in a free society. The proper purpose of a government, Rand shows, is to protect individual rights from the initiation of physical force.

"The Lessons of Vietnam" in *The Voice of Reason: Essays in Objectivist Thought* by Ayn Rand

"The Vietnam war is one of the most disastrous foreign-policy failures in U.S. history," wrote Ayn Rand. In this essay, she analyzes the intellectual bankruptcy behind the Vietnam war, and draws wider, enduring lessons from it.

"The Roots of War" by Ayn Rand

By the nature of its basic principles and interests, laissez-faire capitalism "is the only system that is fundamentally opposed to war," Ayn Rand observes. "If men want to oppose war," she argues, "it is statism that they must oppose."

The Foreign Policy of Self-Interest: A Moral Ideal for America
by Peter Schwartz

This book advocates an approach to foreign policy based on Ayn Rand's morality of rational self-interest, under which our nation's self-interests are measured by only one standard: the individual liberty of its citizens.

Winning the Unwinnable War: America's Self-Crippled Response to Islamic Terrorism, edited by Elan Journo

This book shows how our own policy ideas led to 9/11 and then crippled our response in the Middle East. Only by radically rethinking our foreign policy can we achieve victory over the enemy that attacked us on 9/11; we need a foreign policy based on Ayn Rand's morality of rational self-interest.

Defending Free Speech, edited by Steve Simpson

This hard-hitting collection reveals how the attacks on free speech are the product of destructive ideas—ideas that are eroding Western culture at its foundation. The book exposes those ideas and the individuals who hold them, and, importantly, it identifies the only ideas on which Western civilization can be sustained: reason, egoism and individual rights.

Watch

America vs. Americans by Leonard Peikoff (April 21, 2003)

In this talk Leonard Peikoff analyzes and rejects—as appeasement-ridden and ineffectual—the entire George W. Bush administration response to the terrorist attacks on the United States, from 9/11 through early 2003. America should have reacted to 9/11 as it did to Pearl Harbor, by waging a real war—a merciless war—not on Afghanistan or Iraq, but on Iran: the ideological fountainhead of Islamic totalitarianism.

The Failure of the Homeland Defense: The Lessons from History by John David Lewis. (Recorded March 23, 2005)

With the creation of the Department of Homeland Security, America has accepted a permanent, institutionalized state of siege on its own soil. In this lecture, John David Lewis examines examples from history and argues that such a policy is suicidal. Rather than bracing against further attacks at home, America should destroy her enemies.

Free Speech and the Danish Cartoons: A Panel Discussion with Yaron Brook (April 11, 2006)

The Danish cartoons depicting Muhammad have sparked a worldwide controversy. Death threats and violent protests have sent the cartoonists into hiding and have had the intended effect of stifling freedom of expression. This unflinching discussion—which includes an unveiling of the cartoons—addresses key questions, including: Why is it so important to hold events like this? What is freedom of speech? Does it include the right to offend? What is the significance of the worldwide Islamic reaction to the cartoons? How should Western governments have responded to this incident? How should the Western media have responded?

9/11—A Decade Later—Lessons for the Future (September 8, 2011)

This conference featured three wide-ranging panel discussions:

    Panel 1: "Upheavals in the Middle East: Assessing the Political Landscape"

    Panel 2: "The Islamist Threat: From AfPak to *Jyllands-Posten* and Times Square"

    Panel 3: "Iran, Israel, and the West"

Freedom of Speech or Tyranny of Silence? (January 21, 2015)

Following the massacre of journalists at *Charlie Hebdo* in Paris and a growing climate of self-censorship, this panel opens up a conversation on the future of the freedom of speech. In the discussion, Onkar Ghate talks about the meaning of the right to free speech, the "exceptions" to free speech, the relation between faith and force, and the need for the separation of church and state. The panel includes Flemming Rose, Harvey Silverglate, Jeff Jacoby and Gregory Salmieri.

The Jihadist Movement by Elan Journo (July 2015)

What motivates the jihadist movement? Pushing back against the dominant perspectives on the issue, Elan Journo shows that the Islamist movement is fundamentally animated by a religious goal of subjugation and conquest.

The Israeli/Palestinian Conflict by Elan Journo (July 2015)

What is at the core of the Israeli/Palestinian conflict? Why has the conflict come to seem intractable? What, if any, is America's stake in it? By exploring key elements of the Israeli/Palestinian conflict, this talk by Elan Journo makes a forbidding, convoluted subject lucid.

***Charlie Hebdo*, the West and the Need to Ridicule Religion**
by Onkar Ghate (July 2015)

Attacks like the one against the newspaper *Charlie Hebdo* in Paris are becoming all too common. The Islamic totalitarian threat goes all the way back to 1989 with Ayatollah Khomeini's fatwa against Salman Rushdie. In this talk, Onkar Ghate explains why and how to defend freedom of speech in the face of religious attacks.

Listen

Faith and Force: The Destroyers of the Modern World by Ayn Rand (1960)
The twentieth century was bloody, with two world wars and dictatorships arising around the globe. What is the deepest cause of this warfare and destruction? In this talk, Ayn Rand identifies the cause in our intellectuals' rejection of reason in favor of faith and the morality of altruism. Only by rejecting faith and altruism and embracing reason and a new morality of rational egoism will freedom and peaceful co-existence be possible.

The Wreckage of the Consensus by Ayn Rand (1967)
In this 1967 lecture delivered at Boston's Ford Hall Forum, Ayn Rand questions the morality of fighting a war in Vietnam that "does not serve any national interest." Rand also explains how the military draft violates the rights of those conscripted.

Global Balkanization by Ayn Rand (1977)
Drawing her title from the Balkan Peninsula, where ethnic groups have splintered and warred against each other for centuries, Ayn Rand argues in this Ford Hall Forum lecture that the global trend toward political organization based on race, language and religion bodes ill for the future of Western civilization.

Freedom of Speech, "Islamophobia," and the Cartoons Crisis [Podcast] by Elan Journo (December 18, 2014)
In this podcast, Elan Journo interviews Flemming Rose about his new book, *The Tyranny of Silence*, which explores the Danish cartoons crisis, the reaction to it, and the future of free speech. The interview covers questions such as: What incidents prompted the commissioning of the cartoons? What lies behind the push to outlaw "defamation of religion"? Why is the invalid term "Islamophobia" so destructive?

The Yaron Brook Show: **Freedom of Speech and the Muhammad Drawings**
In this special episode, guest host Onkar Ghate analyzes the appeasing, victim-blaming attitude among many intellectuals toward the Islamist attack on a cartoon contest in Garland, Texas.

Speak Up

Three Things You Can Do Right Now . . .

1. Contribute to ARI

The book you are holding—like all the content and projects of the Ayn Rand Institute—was made possible thanks to the many individuals, foundations and corporations whose financial contributions fund our work. Your contribution will multiply ARI's impact and help fuel our mission to make people aware of the philosophy of Objectivism and its crucial value to human life.

To donate online and to learn about convenient ways to sustain ARI's work, please visit **AynRand.org/support**.

2. Recommend This Book

- Write a review of this book on Amazon.com.

- In conversations, let people know what you found illuminating in this book and encourage them to read it.

- Give away copies of this book (and *Winning the Unwinnable War*) to five of your friends.

3. Tell Three (or 3,000) People

- Engage people in conversation about American foreign policy, correct their misconceptions by pointing to the actual facts of Washington's self-crippled approach, and encourage them to question the basic assumptions shaping U.S. policy.

- Write op-eds, letters to the editor and blog posts to express your view and to indicate the proper ideals that should guide our foreign policy.

- Many of the articles and blog posts in this book are available on ARI's website; share them with your friends on social media.

About the Contributors

Onkar Ghate

Onkar Ghate is the Chief Content Officer and a senior fellow at the Ayn Rand Institute. He is the Institute's resident expert on Objectivism and serves as its senior trainer and editor. For more than a decade, he has taught philosophy at the Institute's Objectivist Academic Center.

Ghate is a contributing author to a number of books on Rand's fiction and philosophy, including *Essays on Ayn Rand's "The Fountainhead"*; *Essays on Ayn Rand's "Atlas Shrugged"*; *Why Businessmen Need Philosophy: The Capitalist's Guide to the Ideas Behind Ayn Rand's "Atlas Shrugged"*; *Concepts and Their Role in Knowledge: Reflections on Objectivist Epistemology*; and *A Companion to Ayn Rand* (Blackwell Companions to Philosophy).

His op-eds have appeared in venues across the ideological spectrum, from *Huffington Post* to CNN.com to FoxNews.com and Businessweek .com. He's been interviewed on national and international radio, including NPR and BBC Radio, and has appeared as a television guest on CNBC, KCET, Fox News Channel and the *CBS Evening News*.

A Canadian citizen, Onkar studied economics and philosophy as an undergraduate student at the University of Toronto and worked in the financial industry prior to joining ARI in 2000. He received his doctorate in philosophy in 1998 from the University of Calgary.

Elan Journo

Elan Journo is a fellow and director of Policy Research at the Ayn Rand Institute. He writes and speaks for ARI, is a senior editor and teaches at the Objectivist Academic Center. He leads the Junior Fellows Program in Policy Research and Legal Studies.

Journo specializes in the application of Rand's ethics of rational egoism to public policy issues. His research and writing focus on the intersection of moral ideas and American foreign policy. His 2009 book, *Winning the Unwinnable War: America's Self-Crippled Response to Islamic Totalitarianism*, analyzes post-9/11 U.S. foreign policy from the perspective of Rand's philosophy. His upcoming book examines American policy toward the Israeli/Palestinian conflict.

Elan's articles have appeared in *Foreign Policy, Claremont Review of Books, Journal of International Security Affairs, Middle East Quarterly,* and in many popular media outlets, including FoxNews.com, *Los Angeles Times, Chicago Sun-Times, The Federalist,* Australia's *Herald Sun* and Canada's *Globe and Mail.* He has been interviewed on Fox News Channel, PBS, NPR and hundreds of radio programs nationally and internationally. Journo briefs congressional staffers and speaks regularly at conferences and university campuses, including Stanford, Berkeley, UCLA, New York University, George Mason University and the U.S. Naval Academy.

Born in Israel, Elan grew up and was educated in the United Kingdom before moving to the United States. He holds a BA in philosophy from King's College, London, and an MA in diplomacy from SOAS, University of London.

Find him on Twitter: @elanjourno.

Leonard Peikoff

Leonard Peikoff has spent more than sixty years studying, teaching and applying the philosophy of Ayn Rand. Having been Rand's foremost student, he is today the world's preeminent expert on Objectivism.

A great admirer of *The Fountainhead,* he first met Rand in 1951, when he was, in his own words, "an ignorant, intelligent seventeen-year-old." He read *Atlas Shrugged* in manuscript and was invited "to ask the author all the questions I wished about her ideas." For thirty years, Rand was his mentor, editor and friend. "We talked philosophy late into the night on countless occasions," he recalls. "It was, for me, an invaluable education." On her death in 1982, Rand named Peikoff heir to her estate.

Born in Winnipeg, Canada, in 1933 (but now a U.S. citizen), Peikoff studied philosophy at New York University and taught at several colleges and universities between 1957 and 1973. For decades he lectured on Objectivism to worldwide audiences through live appearances and audio transcription of his courses. His 1976 course on Objectivism's entire theoretical structure earned Rand's endorsement (she also participated in some of the Q&A periods) and became the basis for his book *Objectivism: The Philosophy of Ayn Rand* (1991), the first systematic presentation of her philosophy.

Peikoff is also the author of *The Ominous Parallels: The End of Freedom in America* (1983); *The DIM Hypothesis: Why the Lights of the West Are Going Out* (2012); and *The Cause of Hitler's Germany* (2014, excerpted from *The Ominous Parallels*).

Asked once to name his life's greatest achievement, Peikoff said: "I mastered Objectivism and presented it to the world."

Yaron Brook

Yaron Brook is executive director of the Ayn Rand Institute.

Brook is coauthor, with Don Watkins, of the national best-seller *Free Market Revolution: How Ayn Rand's Ideas Can End Big Government*. They now have a new book, *Equal Is Unfair: America's Misguided Fight Against Income Inequality*.

He is the host of *The Yaron Brook Show*, a live BlogTalkRadio podcast airing Saturdays, 11:30 a.m. to 1:00 p.m. PT, as well as host of *The Yaron Brook Show* on AM560 The Answer in Chicago, airing Saturdays from 2:00 to 3:00 p.m. PT. He is an internationally sought-after speaker and debater.

He was a columnist at Forbes.com, and his articles have been featured in the *Wall Street Journal, USA Today, Investor's Business Daily* and many other publications. He is a frequent guest on national radio and television programs and is a contributing author to *Neoconservatism: An Obituary for an Idea*; *Winning the Unwinnable War: America's Self-Crippled Response to Islamic Totalitarianism*; and *Big Tent: The Story of the Conservative Revolution—As Told by the Thinkers and Doers Who Made It Happen*.

Brook was born and raised in Israel. He served as a first sergeant in Israeli military intelligence and earned a BSc in civil engineering from Technion-Israel Institute of Technology in Haifa, Israel. In 1987 he moved to the United States where he received his MBA and PhD in finance from the University of Texas at Austin; he became an American citizen in 2003. For seven years he was an award-winning finance professor at Santa Clara University, and in 1998 he cofounded BH Equity Research, a private equity and hedge fund manager, of which he is managing director and chairman.

He serves on the boards of the Ayn Rand Institute, the Clemson Institute for the Study of Capitalism and CEHE (Center for Excellence in Higher Education), and he is a member of the Association of Private Enterprise Education and the Mont Pelerin Society.

Keith Lockitch

Keith Lockitch is the vice president of Educational Programs and a fellow at the Ayn Rand Institute. He oversees all of the Institute's educational programs, including free books to teachers, essay contests on Rand's novels, campus clubs, ARI Campus, the Objectivist Academic Center, ObjectivistConferences.com and others.

Lockitch is a senior instructor for ARI's Objectivist Academic Center, where he has been teaching distance-learning courses on written and oral communication skills for more than ten years. He also teaches classes on Ayn Rand's novels and ideas in a variety of settings, from high school and college classrooms to ARI's internship program to ARI Campus.

As an Institute fellow, Lockitch writes, speaks and serves as a senior editor for ARI. He specializes in the application of Ayn Rand's philosophy to scientific topics, in particular to environmental issues such as energy and climate. His writings have appeared in such publications as *The Daily Caller, Washington Times, Orange County Register, Pittsburgh Tribune-Review, Canberra Times, San Francisco Chronicle* and the science policy journal *Energy and Environment*. He is also a contributor to *Why Businessmen Need Philosophy: The Capitalist's Guide to the Ideas Behind Ayn Rand's "Atlas Shrugged."*

Lockitch received his PhD in physics from the University of Wisconsin, Milwaukee, and prior to joining ARI he conducted postdoctoral research in relativistic astrophysics.

Acknowledgments

We wish to thank Rikki Nedelkow, Simon Federman, Donna Montrezza, Chris Locke, Keith Lockitch, Richard Ralston, Thomas Bowden, Amanda Maxham, Melissa Pranger, Steven Dougherty and Lew Hendrickson. Carl Svanberg, Grant Parker and Christopher Machold assisted in the preparation of the manuscript. Steve Simpson offered valuable editorial feedback on the project.

* * *

This book was made possible thanks to the many individuals, foundations and corporations whose financial contributions fund the work of the Ayn Rand Institute.

About the Ayn Rand Institute

The Ayn Rand Institute believes that your own happiness is the moral purpose of your life, that productive achievement is your noblest activity and that reason is your only absolute. ARI challenges people to rethink their convictions from the ground up and to call into question the philosophical ideas and moral ideals that dominate the world today. By increasing awareness of Ayn Rand and understanding of her revolutionary ideas, ARI continues to make significant strides toward the ambitious goal of changing the culture.

Stay in Touch.

Subscribe to receive timely updates. You'll be the first to learn about our latest initiatives and program successes and how you can help ARI achieve its mission to spearhead a cultural renaissance of reason, rational self-interest, individual rights and laissez-faire capitalism. Now more than ever, it's an exciting time to engage with ARI.

AynRand.org/signup

Selected Books by ARI Intellectuals

The following are some notable books that Objectivist intellectuals affiliated with ARI have written or contributed chapters to. You'll notice that the books vary considerably in their subject, scope and audience. From free speech and foreign policy to welfare entitlements and ethical theory; from the theory of knowledge to philosophy's impact on history and in the boardroom: these books reflect ARI's philosophic outlook and the breadth of our intellectual concerns.

Defending Free Speech
Edited by Steve Simpson (Ayn Rand Institute, 2016)

Equal Is Unfair: America's Misguided Fight Against Income Inequality
By Don Watkins and Yaron Brook (St. Martin's Press, 2016)

A Companion to Ayn Rand
Edited by Allan Gotthelf and Gregory Salmieri (Wiley-Blackwell, 2016)

Judicial Review in an Objective Legal System
By Tara Smith (Cambridge University Press, 2015)

In Defense of Selfishness: Why the Code of Self-Sacrifice Is Unjust and Destructive
By Peter Schwartz (St. Martin's Press, 2015)

The Cause of Hitler's Germany
By Leonard Peikoff (Plume, 2014)

Rooseveltcare: How Social Security Is Sabotaging the Land of Self-Reliance
By Don Watkins (Ayn Rand Institute Press, 2014)

How We Know: Epistemology on an Objectivist Foundation
By Harry Binswanger (TOF Publications, 2013)

The DIM Hypothesis: Why the Lights of the West Are Going Out
By Leonard Peikoff (NAL, 2013)

**Concepts and Their Role in Knowledge: Reflections on Objectivist Epistemology
(Ayn Rand Society Philosophical Studies)**
Edited by Allan Gotthelf and James G. Lennox (University of Pittsburgh Press, 2013)

Free Market Revolution: How Ayn Rand's Ideas Can End Big Government
By Yaron Brook and Don Watkins (Palgrave Macmillan, 2012)

Why Businessmen Need Philosophy: The Capitalist's Guide to the Ideas Behind Ayn Rand's "Atlas Shrugged"
Edited by Debi Ghate and Richard E. Ralston (New American Library, 2011)

Essays on Ayn Rand's "Atlas Shrugged"
Edited by Robert Mayhew (Lexington Books, 2009)

Ayn Rand's Normative Ethics: The Virtuous Egoist
By Tara Smith (Cambridge University Press, 2006)

The Foreign Policy of Self-Interest: A Moral Ideal for America
By Peter Schwartz (Ayn Rand Institute Press, 2004)

Made in the USA
San Bernardino, CA
18 August 2016